Twentieth Century Composers
VOLUME IV

France, Italy and Spain

Twentieth Century
Composers

Edited by
Nicolas Nabokov and Anna Kallin

Twentieth Century Composers

VOLUME IV

France, Italy and Spain

Frederick Goldbeck

WITH AN INTRODUCTION BY
NICOLAS NABOKOV

Weidenfeld and Nicolson
London

First published in Great Britain in
1974 by George Weidenfeld and
Nicolson Limited

ISBN 0 297 76793 3

Printed in Great Britain by
Willmer Brothers Limited, Birkenhead

Contents

To Anne and William

The illustrations are by Kathy Toma, apart from the drawing of D'Indy, which is by Fauré, and those of Roussel and Dallapiccola, which are by Marc Pincherle.

Introduction
The Latin Realm of
Twentieth Century Europe

BY NICOLAS NABOKOV

It stands as a matter of course that the views, opinions and thoughts
as expressed in this volume are those of its author, not of its editors.
This truism would have been superfluous (I have mentioned it once
already in my preface to the first volume of this anthological series)
had those thoughts, views and opinions not been as personal – that
is as unconventional, unexpected, at times iconoclastic and at other
times perceptively original – as those of Fred Goldbeck.

F. G.'s style is peppered with aphorisms, epigrammatic state-
ments, whimsical analogies, excursions into literary metaphors and
similes. He shuns the tenets of technical lingo yet his scholarly
erudition remains unimpaired. As a result his book is pleasantly
readable, instructive, and provocative.

In a way, either consciously or unconsciously, F. G. attempts to
revive the straightforward, ironic and amusing way of talking
about music that was Constant Lambert's in his brilliant *Music
Ho!*. Whether he succeeds or not it is not for me but for the reader
to judge. I for one am pleased that his book is devoid of Beckmes-
serian philistinism or Baedeckerian pedantry. F. G.'s task was
not an easy one. To bring under one hat the different components
of the 'Latin Realm' of Europe (France, Italy, Spain) was difficult
and tricky – if alone for the fact that Paris is included in this

realm. And Paris, as everyone knows, can be substituted not only for the rest of France but also for Western Europe and even America (at least in musical affairs). For over twenty-five of the first crucial years of this century it threw its shadow all over the world. It was Europe's greatest artistic Megalopolis and dictated its tastes to the rest of the Western World, except for those few who in one way or another did not follow the '*gusto francese*'.

Even more significant is the fact that Paris housed, or was at least a centre of activity for such cosmopolitan shapers of twentieth century music as Debussy, Stravinsky, Manuel de Falla, Satie, Prokofiev and Ravel (and a host of other composers of various nationalities and qualifications).

All this overshadowed the Italian and the Spanish scene. Then, of course, each of the countries of the 'Latin Realm' of Europe had a different historical background and different musical traditions. Italy – an uninterupted musical *continuum* since the Middle Ages; Spain – no continuity, with a belated exploration of native, highly polluted folk-lore; France – a sporadic surfacing from the deep waters of one of Europe's most ancient musical traditions, of sacred monsters such as Couperin the Great, Rameau, Berlioz, Bizet and Debussy (I discount, of course, the numberless mini-masters of those odious seventeenth – eighteenth century French maxi-courts and the faded glories of many others.) And here, I believe, F. G. has succeeded in his overall task. He is right, I believe, in ascribing crucial significance to the work of Claude Debussy. No-one nowadays will deny that what the author calls 'Debussy's quiet revolution' was one of the starting points of our century's music. In a way Debussy's 'quiet revolution' was to the twentieth century what Beethoven's very 'loud' one was to the nineteenth century. In this context F. G. has found one especially felicitous remark about Debussy. He calls him '*The emancipator of the consonance*' (as opposed to the various nineteenth century and twentieth century 'Mitropa-oid' emancipators of the dissonance). On the surface it sounds like an aphoristic (and antinomic) calembour. But under the surface of the aphorism is a deep understanding of reality, of the nature of Debussy's music and of its influence upon other composers of this century. Equally felicitous in my opinion are his remarks about the post-Second-World-War 'happenings' on the Parisian scene, especially his appraisal of the work of Boulez and Xenakis and the impact it has exercised upon the music of their younger contemporaries.

All in all this book is readable, enjoyable, clever and accessible to everyone concerned with the life of twentieth-century music. Now F. G. speaks for himself.

Prelude

The nineteenth century prelude to French twentieth century music resembles 'the curious incident of the dog at night time': there was no prelude – although there could have been one. For Berlioz, first of the moderns, was never acknowledged as such by Debussy or Ravel, no more than by Stravinsky. Bizet's *Carmen*, probably the only traditional nineteenth century opera that does not pale by comparison with *Rigoletto* or *La Traviata*, was never extolled by any French musician, as it was by Nietzsche, as a liberating 'mediterraneanizer' of music. Chabrier on the other hand *was* extolled, by composers as different in taste and outlook as Ravel, Kœchlin and Les Six. But, remarkable for a few harmonic and many humoristic *trouvailles*, he foreshadowed none of Debussy's or Ravel's inventions, though he seems to have announced some of the minor masterpieces to come: Poulenc's best, for instance, or *Angélique*, that excellent and most vivid operatic joke – the one hit among Jacques Ibert's (1890–1962) many elegant but too often unblushingly derivative scores.

On the whole the French nineteenth century music that counts has been written by operatic, and nothing but operatic, composers. To Verdi we owe a miraculous Requiem, a fascinating string quartet, and prophetic *Pezzi Sacri*. Gounod wrote half-rheotorical masses and half-meretricious oratorios, Bizet indifferent piano variations and a Mendelssohnian symphony of no greater depth than Saint-Saëns's, and Massenet a ludicrous piano concerto. Such was the state of musical affairs in France when one French composer decided to revise it single-handed, and to make French music abjure the frivolities of footlights, stage-machinery, ballet, and *bel*

1

canto, and grow serious, and even austere and metaphysical.

Vincent D'Indy (1851-1931), whose ancestors had been landed gentry and soldiers, was a militant nationalist and Roman Catholic but by no means a narrow-minded man. The first to edit and perform Monteverde in France, he at once spotted the value of *Pelléas*. But the French patriot chose Wagner for his god, Wagnerian César Franck, a Belgian of German origin, for his master, and the *Sinfonia Eroica* for the best of all possible models of composition. The Roman Catholic Monteverde admirer unceasingly referred to the prototypes of sacred music and tonal polyphony set by Bach whom – probably for being calm and unrevolutionary – he called 'a protestant by mistake'. In his textbooks of composition and in his teaching at the Schola Cantorum, founded to oppose the Meyerbeer-, Delibes- and Auber-ridden Conservatoire, D'Indy's principles were explained and maintained with unflinching doctrinairism: symphonic architecture had to be sonata form, development, 'amplifying variation', and nothing else. Everything had to be as it were organically generated out of a few 'thematic cells', which unfold 'cyclically' in the symphony's or sonata's different sections. As a musical nationalist he could not but commend the use of traditional melodies, from Auvergne or other French provinces, as 'thematic material'. But these traditional songs, introduced into symphony, development, and mercilessly tonal – instead of their native modal – surroundings always look (as Debussy remarked) like charming peasant girls unbecomingly clad in town-dwellers' Sunday best: the follower of Bach's, Beethoven's and Wagner's D'Indy had once and for ever decided to be, prevented him from attempting to shape national and traditional elements of music into some specifically French musical forms – in other words prevented him from being a French Vaughan Williams, Bartók or De Falla.

Busoni liked to quote a popular Italian truism about 'followers who as long as they remain followers have little chance of getting beyond those they follow'. Nothing else is wrong with D'Indy's symphonies, sonatas, and music dramas. For it is difficult to see why D'Indy's always manly and gentlemanly scores should be disdained by those who approve of Bruckner, and of other neogothic achievements of Romanticism in decline. Moreover, at the end of his career, in 1928, D'Indy, quite logically in the line of his Wagnerian heritage and tendencies, but in the teeth of his other ideals, wrote a very strange, and strangely moving short piece: a two-part madrigal for voice and cello, set to words by a Renaissance poet, and which, at the limit of tonal chromaticism, turned out to be, twenty years before Leibowitz and Boulez, the first French counterpart of Viennese atonalism.

Vincent D'Indy's and his Schola's influence has been great and far-reaching. In France he had not only orthodox scholists' like Chausson and Duparc for his disciples, but also Dukas and Roussel. With several grains of paradox, even Satie passed through the Schola, by way of the hyper-Wagnerite Sar Peladan. And between 1890 and 1910 hosts of young composers from Belgium, Switzerland, Greece, Spain, Portugal and South America applied to d'Indy, the master of all the traditions of latterday Romanticism considered as modernism.

But those were exactly the traditions Debussy's inconspicuous revolution was going to make away with.

D'Indy

Debussy

1 Debussy

Monsieur Croche and Copernicus

Music has rarely tried, and always failed, to do without tradition. New scores are made out of elements found in old scores, recent or remote. No composer has ever dealt with harmony, counterpoint, fugue or sonata form without dealing with tradition. But an additional and unprecedented tradition entered the musical scene in Beethoven's day and has since imposed its command on every maker of romantic music: the tradition of anti-traditionalism. All composers, henceforth, agreed to obey the law of disobedience; to break the rules followed by their predecessors and laid down in the textbooks; to favour 'forbidden' dissonances, 'forbidden' sequences of chords and distorted musical structures. For these were the musical symbols of extra-musical claims, such as Beethoven's rebellion against destiny, Schumann's against the Philistines, Chopin's against the invaders of his country, Liszt's against academicism, and Wagner's against the 'old contracts' that fettered Wotan and the others.

Claude Debussy too, born in 1862 at Saint Germain-en-Laye into a rather untypical petit-bourgeois family – mother somewhat severe, father not a little *bohème* – Debussy too, by 1880, started to protest against most things Guiraud tried to teach him in his composition class at the Paris Conservatoire. And by an extraordinary chance a competent witness stood by to record the undisciplined pupil's discussions with his debonair professor.

Debussy, we are told by Maurice Emmanuel (see page 44) sits down at the piano and plays a whole set of parallel fifths and

5

octaves – a blatant abomination and unconditionally banned in the first chapter of any textbook on harmony.

Guiraud: 'Do you really think that's acceptable?'

Debussy: 'I accept it, and I like and enjoy it. Don't you think it sounds good?'

Guiraud: 'Maybe it doesn't sound too bad. But it's impossible. You know the rules.'

Debussy: 'The only rule I admit is the rule that enjoins pleasing a musician's ear.'

Guiraud had good reason to be taken aback, for this was quite a new attitude and an unheard-of sort of rebellion. The romantics and post-romantics enjoyed, no doubt, the harsh, or weird or otherwise eccentric sounds that were the result of their lawbreaking; but this enjoyment was unessential – a by-product, perhaps a reward, of their revolutionary strife. The essential thing was the strife itself. They wrote dissonance, not to please themselves, and others, but to assert themselves, and shock others. The meaning and value of their dissonance was not its sound-value, but its dramatic and psychological impact. As Nietzsche claimed, they did not seek pleasure and happiness but the fulfilment of their task – the task of delivering a message symbolized by their rebellious music. A message of protest, both musical and extra-musical, was a protest against a hostile world and against the coldness and deadliness of its conventions, musical and moral.

It was against this attitude that Debussy was going to rebel; by instinct and unconsciously at first, but soon consciously and explicitly, though in the style of understatement and non-insistence that befits a rebellion against rebellion.

'... I prefer a few notes played on his flute by an Egyptian shepherd, who is attuned to the surrounding landscape and hears harmonies unknown to our textbooks....'

Quiet and idyllic, Egyptian shepherds have nothing to do with knights errant and other dramatic characters.

'... Ask nobody for advice except the wind that passes and tells us the story of the world....'

Told by the wind this 'story of the world' may well have tragic connotations, but it is not the *Weltgeschichte*, the history of the world, full of revolutionary sound and dialectical fury, as listened to by romantics steeped in Hegel. And Monsieur Croche – that slightly Hoffmannesque and admittedly romantic *Doppel-gänger* called up by Debussy when theorizing about music – described himself as an 'anti-dilettante', an adversary, not of those *che dilette* (who enjoy music) but of those connoisseurs who spend their days deciphering 'musical messages', looking for prophetic or at least philosophic tidings in every score they come across, and maintain, for instance, that Beethoven's greatness resides not so much in his musicianship but in his ethics – in his love of humanity in general and his intolerance of most humans in particular.

Tranquility, stillness, impassiveness, instead of romantic agitation: even an early work of Debussy's, composed in the traditional classico-romantic sonata form, is in this respect characteristic, almost programmatic. In the opening bars of *Prélude à l'après-midi d'un Faune* the flute monody – never mind whether played by an Egyptian shepherd or an Arcadian demigod – means something unprecedented in Western symphony: a lazy sensuous drinking-in of sound, something thoroughly un-romantic and anti-dynamic. Music can never dispense with motion, yet this motive almost achieves the paradox of musical immobility, and seems to translate into music Baudelaire's 'Je hais le mouvement qui déplace les lignes'.

Again this static quality in Debussy is by no means confined to slow movements like *Nuages* or *Sirènes*. Constant Lambert rightly described as static the piano piece paradoxically called *Mouvement*; and so is *Fêtes* with its ghostly pageant coming into sight out of unreality and proceeding towards nowhere. This music is the very negation of musical romanticism, which is by definition dynamic and unceasingly 'on the move' through developments driving towards their climax, towards an ending that has to be the conclusion and catharsis of the musical events leading up to it . . .

Debussy's inconspicuous revolution, therefore, meant much more than simply discarding the 'expressive significance' superimposed on their scores by romantic composers or, worse, into them by imaginative listeners. For – in spite of Wagner's *pro domo* theories and three generations of Beethoven explainers – it appears that the progress of music towards romanticism had been intrinsically musical. Beethoven's dramatic symphony and Wagner's symphonic drama were the logical (as well as the historical) outcome of the tonal cadence: dominants, bottling up tension to be disgorged into long-delayed tonics, were the born challengers of Fate and fomenters of symphonic development. Leading notes (*Notes sensibles*)

7

B

and appoggiaturas, yearning to be resolved on to a neighbouring note, were potential Isoldes long before being turned into Wagner's halftone-ridden heroine. And conversely, if Debussy wanted the surface of his music to be even, tideless and unruffled, it was because his ear and his imagination demanded a musical vocabulary and a musical syntax different from, and opposed to, the Romantics'. He disliked the tonal cadence and its dominant-tonic, tension-relaxation seesaw. To escape from being led by leading notes, he soon turned away from the C major scale – 'Le tyran Ut', as Maurice Emmanuel was going to pillory it – to Gregorian modes with no ascending semitones in key positions. He was the first serious composer of symphonic music since Beethoven not to write a symphony; and he used to call that mainspring of romantic dynamism, the development, 'the laboratory of the Void'. Indeed Debussy's main structural device is not the dynamic flamboyant perpendicular of development, but the horizontal order of setting musical elements side by side like so many classical columns. Hence his taste for juxtaposed perfect triads and the prevalence in his style of consonance over dissonance.

Enfranchisement of the unprepared dissonance had always been the practice, and often the warcry, of romantics and modernists. With Debussy consonance, which after *Tristan* stood in greater need of such enfranchisement, sounds 'modern' for the first time because of the unwonted, often slightly archaic, succession of Debussy's consonant chords. Moreover Debussy has his strange way of making dissonant harmony and polyphony sound static and relaxed, of making them almost sound like consonance. And all this results in a musical idiom no less challenging, no less disconcerting for its first hearers than the Viennese school's onslaught on convention by means of heaping tension upon tension and Major 7th upon Minor 9th.

Consonance, calm, unobtrusiveness, avoidance of the dramatic : because of these characteristics Debussy's image has been misread, and his role in twentieth-century music misunderstood. Music historians, especially (for obvious reasons) those formed or influenced by the Teutonic school, are liable not to consider him as 'really modern' but rather as a passing episode, a side track in modern music, a truce between battles, an interlude between *Tristan* and the return to, and increase of, dissonant aggression with Schoenberg; or, on the other hand, between aggressive post-romantic dissonance and the equally aggressive anti-romantic dissonance of *The Rite of Spring*. It was the inconspicuousness of Debussy's revolution that concealed its import, perhaps even from his own view.

In fact, the radical change of music's aspect in this century was wrought, not by Schoenberg, not by Stravinsky, but by Debussy. The much more shocking innovations of Viennese atonalism were nothing but the Ultima Thule of romanticism, of unrelieved tension and unresolved leading notes. And as to the turmoil of *The Rite of Spring* – in the light of Stravinsky's subsequent styles and scores it appears as an intermezzo: most impressive, much imitated, and easy to imitate, but by no means (whatever the legend) epoch-making.

Whereas Debussy's so discreet upheaval was devastating: it was a Copernican redisposition of the universe of Music. Hitherto the music of the Occident had always centred upon the presence of 'contemporary' composers; and, from Beethoven onwards, upon the psychological and autobiographical 'message' contained in their compositions, and upon the here-and-now achievements of their 'advanced' technique. Composers of the past, whatever their stature, were shelved and forgotten – about 1880 nobody outside the precincts of highly specialized musicology had ever heard of Monteverde – or, at best, respected as brilliant forerunners of their successors. Wagner was naïvely and fully convinced that Beethoven – the Beethoven of the Ninth Symphony – was his forerunner, and that the Wagnerian 'total work of art' was going to supersede every other form of music. Spontini boasted of two chords of his own invention, which he considered to be the last word in dramatic music. In Mahler's opinion *his* symphony embodying his *Weltanschauung* was *the* symphony of our day. And Schumann – by no means a radical – wrote on one occasion that many listeners *still* loved Mozart in their hearts: implying that in 1840 the light of even the greatest of eighteenth-century composers could not but be fast fading.

In sharp contrast to this romantic approach, composition for Debussy was never meant to centre on 'the composer as a symphonic hero here and now' but upon a mythical, or at least far-away, impersonal lodestar: the whole of music: 'La musique est un total de forces éparses . . . une mathématique mystérieuse dont les éléments participent de l'infini . . .' – a totality involving things as

9

remote in time as Rameau and Monteverde operas, mediaeval modes, dancers in Delphi and Egyptian shepherds, and as remote in space as Chinese bells and Javanese gamelans. So much so that Debussy's art owes its specific character and flavour, and often its tragic poignancy, to being haloed and veiled by remoteness and impersonality. It is Beethoven's own Fate that knocks at his symphony's door. Schumann's C major Fantasy is 'a long cry towards Clara'. Wagner cannot but be identified with Tristan, Wotan, and Hans Sachs. Whereas in Debussy's opera every character is a figure of remoteness: Mélisande who, when asked about her age, answers 'I am beginning to feel cold'; Pelléas, always on the brink of going away; Golaud, cut off from reality for being insensitive; Arkel, out of reach for being old. *La Mer* and *Ce qu'a vu le vent d'Ouest*, those most realistic seascapes, were not drawn by an old mariner – nor by a frustrated inlander who dreamed of being an old mariner. They were drawn after the eighteenth-century Hokusai's *Wave*, and by Claude Debussy wearing a black coat and a bowler hat. And the eclogue of *L'Après-midi d'un Faune*, after Mallarmé, was set to music by the same impenitent town-dweller whom we can hardly imagine barelegged, let alone clovenfooted.

Debussy's biography, therefore, is of little avail for explaining Debussy's art. To find out that Schumann and Liszt were very lovable human beings and Wagner a very unprepossessing one, may not induce everybody to like Schumann's and Liszt's music, or dislike Wagner's. Yet the human qualities of these romantics had an unmistakable bearing on the musical quality of almost every bar they wrote. But with Debussy we should not let ourselves be tempted to follow the example of the romantics' biographers. For as soon as we delve into the complexities of his two marriages, learn about his callousness when the first broke up, and read the rather maudlin love letters (so strangely out of keeping with his habitual reserve) addressed to his second wife, we feel guilty of eavesdropping without the excuse of solving the secrets of the artist by intruding upon the privacy of the man. To enquire whether or not Debussy was a nice fellow is as irrelevant as asking the same question about Monteverde or Purcell, who expressed in their work only that part of themselves that is impervious to anecdote and contingency. True, '*La Boîte à joujoux* and *Children's Corner* owe their style and their substance to Debussy's tenderness for his little daughter; yet it was again the spirit of remoteness that made him find musical subject-matter in the childlike and the naïve. And once more remoteness has shaped the style – very much resembling his music's – of his correspondence with P. T. Toulet: both friends were touchily unwilling to take and touchingly reluctant to offer advice, even when Toulet's blatant and absurd mishandling of his health impelled Debussy to overcome his reluctance and implore Toulet not to destroy himself – an entreaty, of course, destined to meet with no response.

Nationalism and beyond

'Claude Debussy, musicien français' is the designation printed on the title page of Debussy's last works and also a temptation to be led astray and over-simplify the Debussy case. A strong temptation, for who would doubt his Frenchness? The perfect black triad of beard, coat and bowler hat is his passport, and so is his style of living, first as an impecunious, and rebellious, *petit-bourgeois*, and later on, after his second marriage, as a well-provided, and rebellious, *grand-bourgeois*. And, long before the First World War, he was a patriot and a nationalist who severely snubbed Edward Grieg for being pro-Dreyfus. Moreover – more important – the temperate luminosity of Île de France permeates *Nuages, Reflets dans l'eau, Rondes de printemps*, the Faun's sylvan dwellings and how many other, non-descriptive, pages of his most typical works. And is not his anti-romanticism, his breaking away from *sinfonia eroica* and from the dialectics (fraught with Hegel) of development, a typical vindication of *l'esprit latin*, of French *clarté et mesure* against Teutonic philosophy and ponderousness? On one side the endless second act of *Tristan*, with the lovers evoking the metaphysical meaning of day and night, and of the conjunction 'and'; on the other side the unexpected brevity of Pelléas and Mélisande's love scene, which derives its poetic intensity from understatement and almost from being matter-of-fact: 'I don't think, Mélisande, that there exists any woman fairer than you . . .' A clearcut and convincing contrast indeed.

And yet French classicism is a facet, not the essence, of Debussy's art. First of all nothing could be more alien to Debussy than the classic ideal of the *Grand Siècle*. Even though his project to set *As You Like It* to music never materialized, his art, hardly ever improvised yet always looking as if it were, owes much to Shake-

speare and nothing to Racine. Nothing in Debussy evokes recti-
linear rows of alexandrines or clipped yew trees. He would have
rejected the straitjacket of the 'dramatic unities' as he rejected the
straitjacket of sonata form. The poets of his choice were modern –
Verlaine, Mallarmé – or old 'classics without classicism', like Villon,
Charles d'Orléans, and Tristan l'Hermite. The author of *Pelléas* was
not a French poet but a Belgian whose leanings were akin to the
pre-Raphaelites': Mélisande might have been a godchild of the
Blessed Damosel, one of the young Debussy's first heroines.

He was as much a Northerner as he was a Frenchman. As often as
the light of Île de France (itself by no means southern), his music
mirrors the mist and clouds of some real or imaginary country not
unlike Scotland or Ireland. *La Mer*, in spite of the legend about the
Îles Sanguinaires, is not the Mediterranean, but emphatically – and
unemphatically – the North Sea. Understatement, so often said to
be Anglo-Saxon, is much more a keynote of his music than Gallic
effervescence. And, at the risk of overstating my case, I would add
that his indeed marvellously effervescent evocations of Anacapri,
Seville (*Iberia*) or Cythera (*L'Isle joyeuse*) are inspired, Norman-
Douglas fashion, by a Northerner's half-ironic, half-nostalgic affinities with the South.

With painter and writers

Ernest Ansermet, that unsurpassed interpreter of Debussy's scores,
once remarked that he would begin to trust the German musicologists' musical instinct and judgement the day they would stop
calling Debussy 'an impressionist'. And German musicologists
might well, without loss of dignity, accept Ansermet's hint, for they
would not have to disown a wrong view, but merely to go beyond a
superficial one.

Only an insensitive or disingenuous listener would, if he had ever
seen a Turner, a Renoir or a Claude Monet, deny that *La Mer*, *Fêtes*
and *Reflets dans l'eau* remind him of these painters: *La Mer*, like
Turner's painting, blends grandeur with haziness, *Fêtes* displays the
sensuality of Renoir's vision and his virtuosity, and *Reflets dans
l'eau* out-Monets Monet with harmonies cooler than white water-
lilies and more transparent than green water. And Debussy, the first
to imagine these impressionist sounds, obtained them by very
simple devices which soon became his imitators' paradise: the

woodwind's loquacity combined with the harp's garrulousness; tonally neutral harmonies, as are those derived from the whole-tone scale – a scale almost as conspicuous and popular a Debussy finger-print as impressionism itself; metres that dispense with squareness, and rhythms that renounce impetus.

Impressionism, Debussy's most conspicuous and least significant mark, is answerable for his mannerisms, not for his style; and Debussy's originality depends no more on these no doubt original mannerisms than any man's uniqueness is revealed by his no doubt unique fingerprints. Whenever in his impressionist pages the essential Debussy appears, it is in spite, not because, of this impressionism. The *Préludes* are perhaps the most striking, and surprising, case in point: performed (as they often are) in batches of two or three, many of them are pleasant period pieces, slightly artificial plants out of Odette Swann's winter-garden. But Book I and Book II, played from beginning to end, are both music of quite a different order – indeed of the highest rank. The *Préludes*, deceptively free and seemingly improvised, are not less cogent as a musical construction than a late Beethoven sonata. At its place in the series of twelve every single piece has a significance none, played by itself, ever offers: between *Ce qu'a vu le vent d'ouest* and *La Sérénade interrompue* – with *Des pas sur la neige* lingering in the listener's memory, and *La danse de Puck* to come, *La fille aux cheveux de lin* differs almost as much from *La fille aux cheveux de lin* as played and beloved, by amateur pianists who hardly know of any other of Debussy's works, as does the opening theme of the *Eroica* from the identical theme in *Bastien et Bastienne*. Impressionism is forgotten; architecture has come into its own again. And if anything warrants Debussy's place as the first among the makers of twentieth-century music, it is this mastery in great musical architecture. Granted baroque architecture, made of juxtaposition; looking (in his own words) 'as though not composed'. An architecture achieved, not in the traditional way by thematic interlinking and structural inter-twining of elements, but by novel, paradoxical and mysterious means.

Anti-romantic Debussy disapproves of the romantic creed that music has – or has to have – 'beyond itself' a dramatic, philosophi-cal significance. He would willingly declare with Nietzsche: '"More than music" – that is no musician's saying!'

But why, then, all these extra-musical terms, literary or pictur-

13

esque, on the front pages of the greater part of Debussy's scores from *L'Après-midi d'un Faune* to *En blanc et noir?* The answer is that these titles are merely decorative. They are never intended to hint at the music's 'other' meaning. And moreover they are decorative designations of decorative music. Debussy, who adored *la divine arabesque,* conferred on decorativeness a dignity quite unforeseen by the romantics, who would have shuddered at the idea that any 'meaningful' work of theirs could appear to be 'merely' decorative. The only nineteenth-century musician who could have influenced Debussy in this respect is Berlioz, that romantically minded but classically inspired composer of great decorative *al fresco* music – and, by the way, the composer of the one great Debussyist piece written before Debussy: the *Queen Mab* Scherzo. But Berlioz did not influence Debussy, who did not like his music very much – perhaps because he knew it only through popular but inadequate, over-romantic, boisterous and vulgar renderings.

Once again, as Paul Dukas said, the influences Debussy chose were the painters and the writers more than any musicians. It is the influence of the poetic arabesque of Mallarmé, who declared that 'poetry is made not out of ideas but out of words', and of the impressionist painters who had just found out – though the great painters had always known – that it is not the accurate representation of historical or sentimental scenes that makes their canvas worth painting and looking at, but the arabesque, the visual rhythm of lines and light extracted from any scene or (later on in abstract painting) from no scene at all. Thus all the advanced and smartly esoteric ideas by which romanticism eventually defeated and overcame itself: symbolism, *l'art pour l'art*, the 'poetic principle' of that Edgar Allan Poe, whose *Fall of the House of Usher* haunted Debussy for years as a potential opera, and whom several generations of French poets took to be the great tempter, teaching them to feel godlike when inventing their 'divine arabesques' – all these ideas and principles are applied to music by Debussy, and echoed even in his fashionably modern-styled handwriting. The symphonic or Wagnerian prophet's pride is humbled by craftsman's pride – or craftsman's modesty; and the composer's ambition confined to the making of arabesques whose divinity consists in being pleasurable and decorative. But when all this is said and done, Debussy's music goes quietly beyond Debussy's doctrine.

No more than with Bach, apropos of whose music Debussy

14

coined the phrase, does the arabesque, however divine, have the last word with Debussy. The tragic feel of loneliness in *La Sérénade interrompue*, and in other translations of Toulouse-Lautrec into music, and the deeper tragedy of ironically deprecated anguish are the motives essential Debussy is made of. But it is the doctrine we have to thank for the style that gives these tragic aspects their point: by making them unproclaimed, unsentimental, and ever veiled.

A slightly enigmatic side of Debussy's dealing with literature – and the more interesting for being so – is his own character: as a writer. It will probably remain unexplained how, during the early nineties, a young musician with less than half a classical education, unused to any but the most conventional ways of expressing himself, and hardly able to pen a line without an offence or two against spelling, grammar or syntax – how this duckling managed to grow up into a swan and become that delightful writer who could well, with Nietzsche, have claimed the merit 'of putting into a paragraph as much as others put – or rather fail to put – into a whole book'. But this kind of self-assertiveness was never to his taste.

I doubt whether any music has ever been more irrelevantly praised or frowned at, even by writers who should have known better, than the finale of Beethoven's Ninth. Whereas Debussy:

Beethoven didn't care twopence about being 'literary'. . . . He was a lover of music. . . . And the *Choral* Symphony was perhaps a gesture of still greater musical pride, and nothing else. . . .

Beethoven wanted this idea [the theme of the finale] to be fraught with its potential development: and of wondrous beauty in itself it is magnificent for the things it foreshadows. There is no example of a more ductile musical idea or of one more triumphantly led whither it is destined to go. It dashes from joy to joy, it seems never to tire, nor to repeat itself: imagine some magical tree suddenly unfolding all its leaves at once. . . .

Recently the Ninth Symphony was given side by side with some reeky *chefs d'œuvre* of Wagner's. Once more Tannhäuser, Siegmund and Lohengrin urged the leitmotiv's claims: old Beethoven's exacting and loyal mastery had no difficulty in triumphing over this sort of high-crested tub-thumping about rather vague commitments. . . .

On Mussorgsky:

He is unique and ever will be: for his art without clichés, without desiccating formulas.

Never has a more refined sensibility expressed itself by simpler means:

it seems to be the doing of some curious savage led by nothing but his emotion to discover step by step what music is about. 'Form' is to him of no use whatever – or rather, the form he resorts to is everchanging to the point of being quite unlike any of the established, so to speak administrative, forms. His music, drawn by light touches, holds together by some mysterious link between them – and by his gift of luminous clearsightedness. Sometimes again Mussorgsky hints at quivering shades that enfold and wring the heart. . . .

And Monsieur Croche speaks:

Look here: if a few great men try, obstinately and severely, to achieve something new in every new work of theirs, it is not so with many others who stick desperately to the sort of thing that has been successful once. I don't care for their adroitness. They are addressed as 'masters'. But that may be, I'm afraid, just an urbane way of getting rid of them, or of finding an excuse for the monotony of their methods. . . .

In short I try to forget about music for fear of being hampered in my quest after unknown music – music I am going to know 'tomorrow'. Why should one remain attached to things one knows too well?

Give me two bars – and I shall know how the whole symphony works, or any other musical story. . . .

Can anything be more deeply moving than to have, by mere chance, unriddled the secret of a man nobody for centuries had known of? To have been the man of such a fate. . . such is the only valid sort of fame.

It would be difficult to improve upon these fragments – that is to say, upon the original French of these fragments – in lightness of touch (rarely without a grain of *gaminerie*), in vividness of description, in finality of judgement. But Monsieur Croche never lets his brilliance run away with him. Several witnesses have told us that Debussy disliked Beethoven's last quartets. In his collected writings there is no trace of this dislike, nor of any debunking of any great music, however uncongenial to him personally. On the contrary: flippant paradoxical Debussy displays, along with his subversive opinions, a surprising amount of commonsense – no small merit in a radical innovator and an astonishing feat in a haunted, artistically unsociable personality.

As to the influences that formed his writing, we know that between 1880 and 1885 during an affair with the fashionable wife of a fashionable architect he went through everything he found on the shelves of their library, including dictionaries;

that a little later he became a close friend of Pierre Louÿs', a poet and a nineties sort of writer, the author of a mildly pornographic

16

novel about a courtesan in Hellenistic Alexandria and of the *Chanson de Bilitis* (set to music by Debussy) – an Ossianesque affair, not devoid of preciosity: love poems, presented as a translation from Greek lyrics;

that he met other writers, including Proust, at the Café Weber and in Paris drawing rooms such as Princess Bibesco's;

that he may have thought of emulating his friend Paul Dukas, who knew of every score worth reading and had read at least as many books; and

that Monsieur Croche was invented after Valéry's *Monsieur Teste,* published 1895. Said Monsieur Teste: 'I have, for twenty years dispensed with books'. (Just as Monsieur Croche would try to forget about music.) 'I have burned my papers. I delete live texts. . . . I remember things at will. The difficulty lies elsewhere: to remember things I shall want tomorrow.'

Such are a few of the traceable contingencies. As to the central fact, it was probably by listening once more to the passing wind's advice that Debussy acquired his mastery as a writer.

Under Eastern eyes

As to musical influences, those to which young Debussy was subject are easy to detect: they were mostly superficial and came more often from frivolous than from serious quarters, a certain distrust of the serious being part of Debussy's anti-romantic make-up. About his friendship with Chausson, a dead-earnest Franckist, he remarked: 'The Toreador's aria will always separate us. . . .' meaning that he, Debussy, was not in the least shocked by a facile lowbrow episode, of which Bizet's best admirers (and perhaps Bizet himself too) were a little ashamed. There is an echo of early Fauré's drawing-roomishness in piano pieces like *Arabesques* or the *Suite bergamasque* (written by a young composer who in those days rarely resisted the temptation of signing 'Achille de Bussy'), and not a few slightly meretricious Massenetisms echo even in *Pelléas.* And there was also mock-unearnest Satie, whom Debussy first loved and later on found disturbing for having discovered, a little ahead of Debussy himself, one or two things about static music and the magic of parallel octaves and fifths.

On the other hand – on the serious side – Franck and his appoggiaturas have left their mark on Debussy's String Quartet. And so have *Tristan* and *Parsifal*, not for their chromaticism and even less for their general aesthetic outlook; but Tristan's monodic *traurige Weise*, and Parsifal's nondescript but pervading exoticism did cast their spell.

However, granted all these marginal influences, the main and lasting musical influence on Debussy was that of the Russians, and the young composer's two visits to Russia (1880 and 1881) were perhaps no less opportune than Beethoven's journey to Vienna had been almost exactly a century earlier. Madame von Meck, Tchaikovsky's eccentric, redoubtable and melancholy Egeria, quite charmed with 'Busik', as she called him, had appointed him her musical secretary and private pianist (to play mainly, if not exclusively, Tchaikovsky) and taken him twice to Russia for sojourns of several weeks, which were to come to an abrupt end when he was found flirting with Madame's youngest daughter. But no more than Busik the philanderer's had Busik the musician's time in Russia been wasted: in Moscow he may or may not have met Borodin and Balakirev, but he certainly met not a few composers, and came across many scores – most probably even more than he admitted having read. André Schaeffner, after thorough investigation, has inferred that Debussy knew pretty well how not to disclose his sources, and that his own declarations about the scores he had studied and the dates when he came to study them, have (to put it mildly) often to be taken with a grain of salt.

In consequence Debussy's approach to opera and to music in general was influenced by *Boris Godunov* at a date considerably earlier than reported by some of Debussy's biographers. And this influence can hardly be overrated: a precedent can be found in Mussorgsky and in Mussorgsky alone for almost every distinctive characteristic in Debussy's style. Both are impassive and impersonal, and refer to (modal) folklore without being 'folkish'. Like Mussorgsky, Debussy does not turn drama into symphony, but lets his opera proceed in a free sequence of scenes which in some instances are scarcely connected. His vocal style, like Mussorgsky's again, is the style not of arias, not of recitative, not of emphatically accented *Sprechgesang*, but a kind of conversational psalmodizing. Like Pimen writing down the events that led to Tsar Boris's rise and fall, Debussy tells us (or at least assumes to tell us) about Golaud, Mélisande and Pelléas in the tones of a well informed but uninvolved chronicler. And such affinities of style and mood are all

18

the more significant in a comparison of ingenuous, none too professional Mussorgsky and sophisticated, masterly Debussy. To maintain that without *Boris, Pelléas* would not have been different amounts to maintaining – not altogether against probability, I admit – that if Mussorgsky had not existed, Debussy would have invented him.

And in 1915, nearly twenty years after setting out to write *Pelléas*, the composer of the *Noël des enfants qui n'ont plus de maisons* was still apt to prolong the Mussorgskian way of neither borrowing from, nor imitating folklore, but summoning up the very magic out of which in primaeval times folklore was made, 'to enfold and wring the heart'.

Another and by no means ingenuous Russian innovator did not, strictly speaking, 'influence' Debussy. But – for the same reasons that attuned him to symbolist and *art-pour-l'art* writers and painters – Debussy shared Serge Diaghilev's taste and genius for blending the baroque with the remote and the adventurous with the ornamental.

Diaghilev, like a character of Dostoevsky's, was emphatically a *gentilhomme russe et citoyen du monde*. Cosmopolitan leanings being uncongenial to patriotic Frenchmen, Claude Debussy would not, yet could, have called himself a composer from France and a musician from everywhere.

All those Near Eastern, Far Eastern or Mediterranean, Arabian-nightish or Andalusian fantasies and phantasmagorias met with in Diaghilev's Ballets-Russes productions are also to be found in Debussy's scores. As far back as 1889, when Debussy heard Javanese music at the Paris World Fair, he had learned how to use exoticism not as his music's occasional fancy dress but as an organic pigment of his music's skin. Diaghilev's dreams came true in such perfect choreographies-without-dancers as are – Venice or Seville – *Masques* or *Iberia*. And finally Diaghilev's baroque was carried to heights hardly ever aimed at in *Le Martyre de Saint Sébastien*, that extraordinary and still enigmatic *chef d'œuvre* (1911).

Towards the same time it was said of Henry James – and the remark was not meant to be disparaging – that he was 'writing more and more about less and less'. Likewise one could say of 'late' Debussy that he knew how to win increasing firmness of style out of increasing brittleness of subject matter. D'Annunzio's text of *Le*

Martyre is almost too easy an object for baiting *fin-de-siècle*, Byzantinizing, rhetorical subtleties, dubious taste and questionable religiosity (the ballet performance was banned by the Archbishop of Paris); a pageant of Oscar Wilde motives: onlookers' ponderings, sadistic rather than spiritual, about false gods and true fervour, while the irresistibly seductive young martyr – impersonated by ephebe-like Ida Rubinstein – paces the burning platform before being tied to the post, a target for the young archers bound to kill the captain they love. But all these blatant fads of poet and libretto dwindle into irrelevancy and are forgotten, as soon as Debussy's music intervenes.

Commenting on *Pelléas*, Vincent d'Indy had spoken of *'un art d'enluminure'*; and this remark applies even more accurately to *Le Martyre*. Who cares about D'Annunzio's involved narrative? It is the opposite pages that count: Debussy's 'illuminative art', his *Riches Heures*, also in the Byzantine manner: hieratic figures, static design filled out in colours of tranquil luminosity against a metallic background of trumpets. A style reminiscent of mystery plays, and also of Monteverde's *Orfeo*. Once again this is vocally and instrumentally *la divine arabesque*, ornamental yet fraught with the muted expression of tragedy in the principal Debussy key – the key of remoteness.

Enter the ghosts

It would be hard to imagine any music that sounds more unlike Beethoven's than Debussy's, yet on two points they resemble each other: each in his time opened a new era of music, and their late styles are similar in significance and have met with a similar fate.

Beethoven, when writing his Ninth Symphony, his last string quartets and piano works, had no longer any use for some of his most striking Beethovenisms – such as the rhetoric of his E flat major and C minor, his absorption with the symmetries of expanded sonata form and his frequent indulging in repetitive wordiness – traits that have no doubt contributed to Beethoven's influence, popular image and lasting success. But by 1820 all that had given place to concentration and to contrasts in quick succession, to ellipses and short-cuts at the risk of seeming eccentricity. And just as Beethoven listeners have long been disappointed with the *Grosse Fuge* or the *Diabelli* Variations for not offering them any of those phrases of immediate appeal like the famous one that made the grenadier cry 'Voilà l'Empereur', so are listeners to *Jeux* – with its thinned-out thematic material (almost atomized to the point of being hardly thematic at all) and its adventurous, apparently disconnected construction – equally deceived for not recognizing their impressionist, sensuous and 'atmospheric' Debussy whom it was so much easier to understand. Again, if Beethoven's deafness was made responsible for the discomforts of the Ninth Symphony's finale, Debussy's illness turned him, at the age of fifty, into a figure almost as isolated as 'old' Beethoven had been, and provided his critics with an explanation of his going to otherwise unaccountable extremes.

And to extremes, indeed, he went, and in different directions. First towards the Jamesian 'less and less'. In *Jeux* and the *Études*, late Debussy is aware of the fact that his melodic and harmonic materials, handed down to the twentieth century through so many classical clarities and romantic obscurities, are threadbare, thinned-out and tired-out materials, that a sort of desperate and uncanny mesmerizing power is required to shape them into one more piece of live, if tardy, music. And there is also Debussy's quasi-Proustian recourse to 'remembrance of things past'.

Copernican Monsieur Croche knows, or at least sensed by musical instinct, that the composer's situation, fate and dignity will never again be the same; that, no longer in the centre, he is in the fringe of musical events; that he can no longer speak up without getting involved in a dialogue with several centuries of Western music. A dialogue not without precedent: Mozart took to Bach in Baron van Swieten's library. Beethoven and Berlioz evoked 'the Lydian mode' and 'the Gothic chant', but Mozart's and Beethoven's exception and Berlioz's once-in-a-while became Debussy's permanent haunt – in fact, the *basso continuo* of his method and composition. An unquiet, ever-shifting base: the Sonata for cello and piano, for example, after a Monteverdean opening, sums up, almost line by line, Mussorgsky, gypsy fiddling, Venetian guitars, Brighton minstrels, other street-singers and what not. And yet no detail is pastiche, nor is the ensemble patchwork. Because every bar is tinged with, and their succession unified by, the pale and pervasive colour of ghostliness – that last word of Debussy remoteness. And this quality, by definition an elusive one, is nevertheless so clearly apparent that pianists know that their hands have to be arched and their keyboards attacked in a particular way to obtain the Debussy touch, which has to be evocative of expression, rather than expressive. The naïvety of that conductor has often and undeservedly been made fun of, who during a rehearsal turned round to ask: 'Now look here, Debussy, you indicated *pp espressivo* . . . but what is it you want – *pp* or *espressivo?* You cannot have it both ways . . . ?'

One probably cannot – short of admitting that *pp espressivo* is the *espressivo* of ghosts.

Awareness – that clear-sightedness Monsieur Croche admired in Mussorgsky – had always been the essence of Debussy's ear and mind. Yet mature Debussy had learned a few things that before had perhaps escaped him: that no amount of anti-romanticism can bring back the halcyon days or revive the tranquil joy of classic utterance; that the preference he gave to the impersonal over romantic self-expression became unavoidably Debussy's personal way of not expressing Debussy; and that no Egyptian shepherd, be he never so expert a flautist, can redeem twentieth-century musicians from their latterday-ness.

Still, aware of all this, Debussy did not recant, but went to explore that phantasmal dimension of music already foreshadowed in much earlier works – as in the pageant of *Fêtes*. He agreed to 'go back' to the romantic sonata, and write one for violin and piano, complete with cyclic unity of theme as postulated by D'Indy: and it turns out to be – in sound and mood – unreal, a ghost-like sonata. And in the war-inspired suite *En blanc et noir*, the ghost of Luther's hymn and the ghost of a song from Île de France appear, as though out of limbo, and clash and combine into an almost terrifying music of burning unreality.

Charles Morgan, commenting upon lateness and modernity, once quoted a few lines written (and then suppressed) by Keats in the draft of one of his poems:

> The feel of not to feel it,
> When there is none to heal it,
> Nor numbed sense to steel it,
> Was never said in rhyme.

Never said in rhyme – but perhaps, and for the first time, said in music: by Claude Debussy. And, after Debussy, no good musical rhymers shall be allowed to disregard the possibilities and impossibilities of a similar pursuit.

2 Ravel

Independence and tradition

Ravel said: 'When as a young child I first felt attracted by music, it was my father, a better musician than most amateurs, who knew how to develop my taste and stimulate my curiosity'. Yet music was not Monsieur Ravel's preoccupation in life: an independent character, he spent all his time and his small income on technical research, and invented, constructed and drove, slightly terrified neighbours watching, a motorcar in the late eighteen sixties. Of Swiss origin (and himself the son of a man of whom we know little more about than that he was unconventional enough not to have cared when some registrar or other civil servant had inadvertently changed his name – Ravet – into Ravel on some passport or other official paper), he left his country for France, stayed for some time in Ciboure, near the Spanish border, and married a Basque girl.

Independence and a taste for experimenting – often along do-it-yourself lines – on his father's side; strong traditional roots, and direct, naïve musicality on his mother's – such are the contradictory elements that account for the dissonances in Ravel's life, and for the paradoxical charm of 'natural artificiality' in Ravel's music.

In 1897 he entered Fauré's composition class at the Paris Conservatoire, and, unlike Debussy, proved not a rebellious but a most attentive and obedient pupil. Yet the Prix de Rome, obtained by undisciplined Debussy, was denied to disciplined Ravel – probably because Debussy's influence, of which the academic jury strongly disapproved, was obvious in several works which had already drawn attention to Ravel's name. His String Quartet is indeed an

23

immediate offspring of Debussy's, and in *Jeux d'eau* pure Debussy harmonies are applied to a new style of piano writing. For it was undoubtedly Ravel who, going beyond Liszt's inventions, dissolved the black and white keyboard into an unprecedented spectrum of colours: first instance of that typical 'impressionist' style of writing for the piano, which Debussy himself was to adopt and adapt in his *Reflets dans l'eau*.

Thanks to Debussy's anti-romanticism and anti-Wagnerism Ravel could at once enter a French musical scene so radically freed from the Teutonic spell that it seemed by now unnecessary to rebel and argue against over-emphasis and longwindedness. His beliefs and his methods were, however, altogether different from Debussy's. While Debussy refused to obey the academic rules, Ravel contended that even the most eccentric experiments could easily be reconciled with the rules; that extension by analogy of the traditional principles entitled him, for example, to settle dissonant chords (previously always rooted in the dominant) on any degree of the scale; and that by resorting to so-called acciaccaturas and other unresolved 'wrong notes', already favoured by a composer as classical as Domenico Scarlatti, twentieth century musicians could make the best of both the orthodox world of unexceptionable harmony and the heretical world of unfamiliar sound.

Remembrance of things past

There is, though, something strangely ironical and fictitious about Ravel's loyalty to academic rules and conventions, which are seemingly obeyed as if they were valid and unchallenged – as if it were natural and easy to produce, with their help and guidance, music 'as of old'. And such had indeed been the fool's paradise cherished by a Saint-Saëns or a Tchaikovsky, who were genuinely convinced that, by keeping to the traditions set by Mozart and Beethoven (or supposed to be set by them), they were going to be composers 'like Mozart or Beethoven'. Ravel on the contrary, whatever tradition he chose to follow (or pretended to follow), knew pretty well how barren, brittle and threadbare, after all the romantic wear-and-tear, those traditions had become. He knew that he was not a classical composer steeped in live tradition, but a tardy though a reminiscent one. 'Remembrance of things past' can, indeed, for a fascinating moment revive defunct forms of musical feeling and thinking. But if Proust never had to aim farther back than his childhood, Ravel's *temps perdu* comprised the entire 'imaginary museum' of history of music, and may be longed and looked for in Liszt's Rome, in Schubert's Vienna, in Couperin's Versailles.

In this, again, Ravel was like Debussy: surrounded by ghosts. And again, unlike Debussy. For Debussy, even in his dealings with ghosts, was led by his fantasy, his dreams and his ear's pleasure. Ravel, much more sceptical and rationalistic, always considered composition to be a sort of conjuring trick, or an exercise in legerdemain. Technique, he maintained, was everything, inspiration nothing. He infuriated music's idealists and moralists by declaring 'that he hated sincerity' – meaning uncontrolled and unsifted musical utterance. Edgar Allan Poe's 'poetic principle' enchanted him. And applied to composition, this meant a piece of music exactly planned and thought out, form and content, style and expression, and then carried out with utter precision; the composer-who-writes being the foreman who has to obey, down to the last screw, the composer-engineer who has, in accordance with old rules, invented a new musical machine destined to amaze, puzzle and fascinate, as did the feats of the once famous mechanical chess player.

The spirit of Ravel's approach to music never changed, nor did his methods. His style, on the other hand, and almost his aesthetics changed with every work he undertook: he never wrote two of the same type. *Daphnis et Chloé* is Russian ballet music in the style of Rimsky-Korsakov, only much more consistent as a symphonic construction. *Gaspard de la Nuit* succeeds in reconciling Debussy's introvert art of evocation with Liszt's extrovert demoniacal virtuosity. *La Valse* and *Valses nobles et sentimentales* are very different images of romantic Vienna. The brilliant *La Valse*, with its pleasantly disquieting *Satan-conduit-le-bal* developments, evokes Johann Strauss's sociable Vienna, galvanized and stylized by means of a sumptuousness of scoring that no Strauss, not even Richard, ever foresaw. *Valses nobles et sentimentales*, much more difficult to perform, and to understand, deals with Schubert: this is Schubert's romanticism, unromantically clad in sophisticated dissonance and lucid virtuosity, and yet a deeply nostalgic quest for Schubert's nostalgia. More than any other musician Ravel seems to have agreed with Schubert's saying about the sadness of every sort of music and the still greater sadness of music meant to be light-hearted.

Hermit about town

In every score, almost every page of Ravel's, whatever his style we come across certain modal melodic patterns which embody this streak of sadness – surprising, and the more significant in a musician so averse to haziness, so little given to elegy, so determined never to let himself go. Ravel was no romantic confessor of his melancholy moods. At least as deliberately as Debussy he wanted his music to be untinged by personal elements. But with Ravel this taste for discretion was singularly encouraged by the elusiveness of his personality. A charming, urbane and sociable, quick-witted and witty man, neither pretentious nor humble, but in all simplicity clearly conscious of being, after Debussy's death the first of French musicians, it fell to his lot to lead an incredibly bleak life. No biographer's inquisitiveness has so far succeeded in discovering that he ever loved any human being except his mother, whose death turned him overnight from a boyish-looking young man into a still youngish-looking and yet prematurely aged one.

As a famous composer and a ready talker he was, of course, much sought after by intelligent admirers and lion-hunters alike. He easily accepted their company as an alternative after all preferable to solitude, and used to call on them at impossibly Proustian times of night; and, relaxing between periods of isolation and grim work on another masterpiece, he was always willing to let them take him to innocent parties at night clubs, where he drank little and danced a lot. For he was a better dancer than musicians usually are, and given to adorning the elegant slimness of his appearance with eccentric ties, waistcoats, socks and spats. But naïve satisfaction about such fantasies and accomplishments did not prevent him from being tacitly unhappy about not being taller by a few inches. To forget this, or perhaps masochistically to rub it in, he had chosen to live at Montfort l'Amaury, in a house as remarkable for the diminutive size of its rooms, as for its pleasant sloping garden, among equally diminutive Siamese kittens and Victorian toys and knick-knacks.

Imitation

It is time to revert to Ravel the composer's dialogue with all sorts of other composers' music, present or past: a dialogue that, in Ravel's view, should always start with imitation. 'Never be ashamed of imitating,' he advised young disciples. 'If your pastiche is, as such, quite successful, nothing is lost. If you don't succeed in being entirely derivative, the difference between your score and the chosen model will show your originality.'

Ravel's own imitations were sometimes very close – or at least intended to be so: the second movement of his Violin Sonata is genuine jazz; its finale and *Tzigane* are photographic portraits of Paganini's, and the Hungarian gypsies' fiddling; and the Left-Hand Piano Concerto culminates in a passage borrowed from a Liszt rhapsody. Sometimes his models were less straightforwardly dealt with: the Adagio of his G major Concerto was composed 'two bars by two bars', he declared, 'exactly after' the slow movement of Mozart's Clarinet Quintet, but I must confess that, hard as I have tried, I have never been able to follow Ravel's method of copying. The result is splendid, but hardly a good pastiche. Likewise, before writing the fugue of *Le Tombeau de Couperin*, Ravel studied, analysed, took to pieces and rewrote the twentieth fugue of Bach's forty-eight. Yet ultimately his own fugue, static and modal, turned out to be the fugue that in mood and in style differs more than any other fugue, ancient or modern, from all the fugues ever written before.

On one occasion at least his imitating was merely assumed, almost imaginary. His *Mallarmé* songs were indeed scored for the same instruments as Schoenberg's *Pierrot lunaire*. But Ravel had neither heard *Pierrot lunaire* nor read its score. He had simply been told about it by Stravinsky, who did attend one of its first performances in Berlin (and was thus able to try his hand at an imitation, *en connaissance de cause*, with his *Japanese Lyrics*). And it is not impossible (it is even probable) that Ravel's bent towards imitation, towards looking for all sorts of models, was in itself an imitation of Stravinsky's similar tendencies.

Ravel had never any qualms about letting himself be influenced by Stravinsky. (Compare the slow movements of Stravinsky's Piano Sonata and of Ravel's G major Concerto: the two pieces may be very different in expression, they are parallel in style.) But I heard him once say – and though intended not to be taken quite seriously, what he said proved his clear-sightedness about both Stravinsky and himself – 'In comparison with myself, Stravinsky's superiority consists in the fact that I am by far the better musician of the two.' By 'being a better musician' Ravel meant his up-bringing at the Paris Conservatoire and his maternal heritage of earthy Iberian musicality. Which had made him less bold, much less disposed to accept those distortions à la Picasso, squinting harmonies, lopsided rhythms and other devious idioms – that came almost as a matter of course to the unhampered Stravinsky.

Puppet-shows and fairy-tales

And yet, as we have said, Ravel's way of conforming to good musician's conventions is always deceptive. With him the academicist's comfortably trodden path appears to be nothing but a short cut towards his particular, enchanting and melancholy and never comfortable domain of aloofness, virtuosity and artificiality. Listening to Ravel means listening, more often than not, to either a musical puppet-show or a musical fairy-tale. There is a touch of unreality about his music's style and atmosphere; not, of course, because puppet-shows and fairy-tales deal with imaginary adventures, but because Ravel uses this technique when addressing, not the childlike and the naïve (for whom 'real' puppet-shows and fairy-tales are made), but the sophisticated and the disillusioned – those who are likely to enjoy mechanical artificiality for mechanical artificiality's sake, and to be moved by fairy-tales, not because of their belief, but because of their disbelief, in fairies.

In accordance with this approach, *L'Heure espagnole*, the first of Ravel's stageworks, is the perfect puppet-show. The mechanical background is provided by the worthy clockmaker's workshop, with its dozens of clocks ticking and striking. The music, a delightful entertainment made up of Spanish rhythms and Italian *bel canto* in parody and in miniature, sounds like a set of variations on Debussy's *Sérénade interrompue*. And the action mainly consists of an extremely patient and muscular muleteer carrying up to and down from Doña Concepción's bedroom the bulkiest of grandfather clocks in the depths of which, each time, an ineffective would-be lover of the poor frustrated lady is hidden. Eventually the young muleteer, who represents the redeeming touch of nature, is invited to ascend, clockless, in his own right.

Marionettes and fairies meet in Ravel's other operatic score, *L'Enfant et les sortilèges*. A little boy, unwilling to learn his lessons, yields to bad temper, goes for the tame squirrel with the point of his pen, lacerates the wallpaper, spoils a precious screen, and is left by his mother to suffer for his sins. Indeed, he is threatened and haunted by the spirit of the fireplace, the respectable armchair, the Wedgwood teapot; by the 'old man of sums', and the arithmetical symbols themselves; and worst of all, he is found unworthy of acting as the knight of the Princess from his story book. At nightfall the beasts in his mother's garden join in rating the culprit. In the heat of the hubbub one of them is wounded by the others. The little boy shows his kindness of heart by dressing, with his handkerchief, its injured paw. Released by the forgiving noises of all, he finds final redemption in his mother's smile. And likewise, the slight Peter-Panishness of this *fantaisie lyrique* is redeemed by Ravel's faultless blending of the spirit of extravaganza with the spirit of poetry. For the cats' duet (which out-Rossinis Rossini), the teapot's 1925 blues, and the arithmetical figures' Czerny-like discourses are episodes far to delicately formed and shaped, far too completely translated into pure musical *scherzi*, not to hold their own side by side with the admirable, never sentimental and ever moving, music of the Fire, the Princess, and the Garden.

It is again its puppet-show aspect – visible wires and angular motion – that accounts for the fascination of *Bolero* (1927), Ravel's first and only popular success – a success which vastly surprised the composer himself.

Nothing could be more mechanical: the identical period fourteen times repeated in ever louder and more flamboyant orchestral colours. Moreover, an intention of parody seems to be implicit: *Bolero* was written in 1928; neo-classicism, the 'return to Mozart and Bach' was rampant in Paris. And Ravel seems to say: 'You want to go back to the eighteenth-century tonics and dominants? *Eh bien*, I am going to give you C major undefiled, and to ram it down your throats for a quarter of an hour in the tempo of an absurdly slowed-down bolero, until, after the jerk of a sudden, unforeseen, and final modulation, you discover in an afterthought, how impatiently you have been waiting for it – and how maddening the whole thing has been!' Maddening – and yet a bit terrifying. We are reminded of Kierkegaard's saying that mechanical evenness superimposed upon human utterance or gesture 'partakes of the demonic'.

Knight errant's vigil and watchmaker's wisdom

There is also something frightening about the interplay between the composer's so impersonal approach to music and the fate of the man. Ravel's last years were darkened by a strange, somehow mechanical disease of his brain. The battery was sound, but the switchboard out of order: his mental powers were not impaired, least of all his judgement and his musicality (the last time I met him, at a rehearsal, I heard him correct a minor mistake, which had escaped everybody else, including the conductor), but his memory failed him more and more. At times he did not remember where he was staying in Paris; it took him minutes to form the letters of his name. Once, at a dinner party talking, as lucidly as ever about his own and others' music, he suddenly puckered his brow and, giving an accurate description of one of his piano works, asked his neighbour to help him out with its title, which happened to be *Gaspard de la Nuit*.

He bore this suffering with pathetic dignity, but – much against his intention – his anguish is mirrored in his last works. Particularly in his Concerto for the Left Hand, through whose shifting jazz rhythms the underlying stiffness of bottled-up despair is unmistakably disclosed – even though the puppets pretend that their angular gait means playfulness and parody, as of old.

In contrast a comforting angel, straight out of a fairy tale, seems to have inspired him in his ultimate composition – the triad of *Don Quixote* Songs – the *Chanson épique*. And for the last time the well-known tranquil, modal and archaic Ravel melody is summoned up, as Don Quixote entreats St Michael and St George to strengthen his arm in Dulcinea's service.

According to Stravinsky, Ravel was 'a Swiss watchmaker among composers'. Quite, but if we want the watchmaker to resemble Ravel, we must look for the wisest and most human; the one who though calmly secure in being the first of his craft, would admit with a smile that he has to be thankful if the perfection of man-made timekeepers is not surpassed by the natural exactitude of the slim dark line that needs neither wheels nor watchmaker's toil to appear on the face of a sundial.

3 Dukas

Unrebellious yet undomesticated

Everything – his style, his methods and his character – had pre-ordained that Dukas should be a great unacknowledged and un-performed composer like Kœchlin, Maurice Emmanuel or Caplet. But the History of Music, that capricious impresario, decreed that he should be a famous and popular one, all through the first half of the twentieth century. Famous and popular, indeed – but only as the composer of *L'Apprenti Sorcier*, written by Paul Dukas, aged thirty-two, in 1897. Two years earlier, Richard Strauss, aged thirty-one, had written *Till Eulenspiegel*, and the two symphonic entertainments are very much in the same vein and style. Descriptive music at its most blatant: the magician's disciple, about to be drowned, is as realistically portrayed as Till about to be hanged. But also descriptive music at its best: whoever disapproves of music's being figurative has only to take these scores as 'just a scherzo' and 'just a rondo' to find them quite enjoyable.

As makers of orchestral scores Dukas and Strauss certainly have a few traits in common. Both were brilliant and most able craftsmen. Both had learned their particularly brilliant technique of scoring from Berlioz rather than from Wagner, and from Liszt rather than Berlioz. And in both, complete technicians though they were, the horse-sense of 'natural' musicians unsophisticated at root is never found wanting. But as makers of music they are most dissimilar. It would have been as difficult for Dukas to be, as for Strauss not to be, trivial and pompous. Strauss had never any doubt about the validity of his style. To win the timber necessary for building ten symphonic and fifteen operatic scores he never went

31

beyond grafting a few twigs of waltzing frivolity upon the branches of Wagner's mythological ash-tree. Whereas Dukas, though no less faithful a Wagnerite, was always aware that the days of this mythological timber were gone, and that one had to build with other material and differently.

Still, among the musicians who took part in the 'unobtrusive revolution', Dukas was no doubt the least revolutionary. Hardly a revolutionary at all – in spite of which his place is clearly marked out, not in the academics' camp, but in Debussy's.

Beyond romanticism by way of Beethoven

He never wrote another *L'Apprenti Sorcier*, thus (it is said) incurring his wife's displeasure, who after having chosen a dashing composer found that she had married an introspective one and the composer of an unmistakeably romantic piano sonata – the last romantic sonata (1902). Romantic, not post-romantic music. For post-romantic music is in general either histrionic or lachrymose, or both, and Dukas's sonata is nothing of the sort. The opening movement is Schumannesque in its dark, impassioned themes and polyphonic layout, the Finale triumphantly Lisztian (in the serious manner of Liszt's own Sonata), the Scherzo a very French toccata interrupted by a strange Trio, which looks, and sounds, almost like Webern. And the late Beethoven is revisited in the long ('much too long', Dukas used to say later on) and austere slow movement: a homage, ringing very true though bordering on pastiche, to the *Hammerklavier* Adagio.

Beethoven again – the Beethoven of the *Diabelli* Variations – stood godfather to Dukas's next work. The *Variations, interlude et finale sur un thème de Rameau* (1903) were in those days deemed 'intellectual', simply because they appeared to be much less romantic than the sonata and much more concise, and a masterpiece of counterpoint as well as of keyboard writing. An extremely pleasant work – particularly for its felicitous and brilliantly intelligent (if not intellectual) blending of scholarly seriousness with decorative elegance and warmth of expression.

In the true Diabelli manner Dukas, having chosen his Rameau minuet for its simplicity and innocence, takes it to bits in one variation, builds it up again in the next and leads it, through all sorts of styles, from Rameau's harpsichord to late Beethoven's violent black-and-white keyboard drawing. Then, by way of romantic colours, Wagner's pre-impressionist *Tarnhelm* harmonies, and even a whiff or two of actual impressionism, he returns to classicism and Rameau, in the *divertissement* of a sweeping *finale*.

Dukas was, of course, quite aware of and exaggeratedly humble about his Beethovenisms. A young pianist, one day, reported that Cortot had advised her to play the *Rameau* Variations and the *Diabelli* at the same recital. 'Better not,' said Dukas, 'unless you want them to say: "Dukas – poor devil . . ."'.

In fact, differences of stature granted, Dukas, writing his variations, was no more Beethoven's 'poor devil' than Stravinsky, writing thirty years later his Mass, was going to be Guillaume de Machaut's. In both cases these twentieth-century composers were not diabolizing, but dialoguizing with music of the past. But by choosing late Beethoven, Dukas – not unwittingly, we may assume – added to the complexity of the situation: in the *Diabelli* Variations, with their allusions to Bach, Handel and Mozart, we find the first foreshadowing of 'reference to the past considered as a device of modernism'. Dukas's choice, therefore, meant accepting a dialogue, at one remove, with another dialogue.

If ever a composer was destined by temperament and equipped by education for this sort of dialogue, it was Dukas. From Obrecht's day up to his own it would be difficult to name a score worth reading that he had not studied. He knew about every technique and every style, and he had a fellow-composer's understanding – different from any musicologist's – of the musical and the extra-musical impulses and conditions that made Palestrina perfect and austere, Donizetti effective and frivolous, Wagner triumphant, and Rameau and Berlioz great and controversial. He was a humanist and a sage, and his looks were a mixture of a mandarin's aristocratic spirituality and a Socrates's spiritualized ugliness. But the aristocrat was easy-going, the spiritualist unassuming, and the ugly sage had a charm about him which the few he wished to please found hard to resist. And the mandarin spotted the exact historical context of every work he came across – spotted and often, in his numerous essays, even pigeonholed the works and their context with a scholar's accuracy, and sometimes with a school-master's relish in wealth of information. Yet always at one moment or another Socrates came in and let his irony and scepticism weigh the work's imponderable aspects and qualities.

No wonder therefore – given this frame of mind – that Dukas's problem ultimately appeared to be the same as Ravel's: the problem of being born under the law of tradition and bound to the law of modernity. And so vivid, so unescapable, was his awareness of this problem and of the *impasse* it was fast leading to, that he had to choose it for the dramatic subject-matter of his next (and last) major work: his opera *Ariane et Barbe-Bleue* (1906).

'Who knows about Ariadne?' (Nietzsche)

The rebellious Ariane is determined to liberate herself and Bluebeard's other wives (who in Maeterlinck's version have not been murdered but imprisoned in the castle). She seeks freedom not from gaol only, but from the traditional law of wives' submission to awe-inspiring husbands. And she succeeds brilliantly. The *seigneur et maître* is not beaten but routed. He is thoroughly and doubly humbled. First Ariane's disobedience has, to his surprise, increased his love for her – such is the glamour of the New Woman who dared resist the beneficiary of fading feudalism. Secondly Ariane saves him from being lynched by his peasants, who, under the spell of Ariane's beauty, have also decided that the days of docility are over. But alas, her very victory means defeat: she discovers that wives, as wives go, have no wish to escape from Bluebeard's authority and Bluebeard's prison; and, worse, that to herself Bluebeard, no longer formidable, is no longer attractive. Nothing is left for her but to bid adieu to Bluebeard, his castle and his love, and to recede into disillusionment and loneliness. Even dismantled, Tradition has won.

Ariane et Barbe-Bleue, with Maeterlinck as its librettist, has had to suffer from comparison with *Pelléas* – the more so, since Dukas in this score appears for the first time as a disciple of his friend Claude Debussy. Static harmony, mostly based on the whole-tone scale and other Debussy devices, stand out. And though no musician guessing at the identity of the composer would attribute to Debussy the enigmatic, modal and archaic *Chant des filles d'Orlamonde*, there is no doubt that without Debussy it could never have been written. Yet there are quite different elements in *Ariane.* Very much unlike *Pelléas*, Dukas's 'fairy-tale in three acts' is symphonic as well as operatic: two decades before *Wozzeck* he gave its first act the strict form of a set of variations. True, these non-Debussy aspects of the score are not always the best. Symphonic construction sometimes entails symphonic redundancy, and Bluebeard now and then seems to share a slightly ominous *air de famille* with Wotan and Hunding. Still, Ariane's last scene is perfect and unprecedented in Dukas. The music that frames Ariane's triumph-of-no-avail goes far to prove that, to open the door of the metaphysical domain, music's purely musical means are a key more likely to fit than the key of philosophy or even the key of wisdom. Dukas has ceased to refer (in the manner of the Sonata and the Variations) to Beethoven's late idiom. And yet it is midway between the Arietta, Op. 111, and the music concluding Busoni's *Doktor Faust* that this last, deeply human yet unearthly scene of Dukas's opera finds its place: for once, the mandarin's mastery of all the secrets of writing has met with the unaccountable promptings of Socrates's *daimonion*.

Like Rossini and beyond Webern

Op. 111, and *Faust* . . . In Thomas Mann's novel *Doktor Faustus* a cranky professor explains how and why Op. 111 meant 'Beethoven's farewell to sonata form'; and Ariane's *Adieu* came near to being Dukas's farewell to composition. During the twenty-nine years he had still to live he published only *La Péri* (1912), written for a successful Russian dancer, for some time his mistress: a most competent ballet score in the pure Franco-Russian and truly impressionist manner, to which, later on, he added a much more interesting opening fanfare for brass; and two admirable occasional compositions: *La Plainte, au loin, du Faune* (1920), a short piano piece in memory of Debussy, and a Ronsard sonnet for voice and piano (1924), a model of good archaizing.

Like Rossini's, Dukas's retreat into silence defies explanation – even by cranky professors. He was never in the least neurotic. Until his short last illness he never suffered from any loss of vitality. Moreover he went on composing but nobody was allowed to see his 'work in progress', and he destroyed every trace of it a few weeks before his death. He certainly had a rare gift for being lazy without feeling guilty. He enjoyed reading, life in general and meeting a few good friends. Taking his celebrity and prestige for granted or perhaps even for undeserved, he never felt frustrated, and was entirely unambitious as far as honours and acknowledgments go.

Asked whether it would give him pleasure to be promoted Com-mandeur de la Légion d'Honneur, he merely remarked that he had always been more at home in Don Giovanni's part than in the Commendatore's and was not going to change.

He liked teaching, and was adored by his pupils, a little like Socrates again, but rather more like Dr Johnson – 'Je n'ai jamais été méchant, mais toujours plutôt ours' – whom he also resembled in his frequent retorts, admitting of no contradiction, in the style of 'No Sir, that will never do: you don't see your way through the question!'

I happened to attend one of his classes when a young man from south-eastern Europe was playing a piano reduction of a string quartet that he had obviously taken great pains to compose. After the last chord and a moment of ominous silence Dukas said, 'Well, you know that this particular form of music appeared in the days of Haydn, that great master. Then came Mozart's most admirable quartets; but the apex of quartet-writing was of course reached with Beethoven. Several quite good romantic quartets followed, and in our time Debussy has written the excellent one you know. And now . . . now this form is dead. Here's your score.' A discourag-ing verdict indeed. And an erroneous one, for while Dukas was signing the quartet's death warrant, Bartók was engaged in proving its splendid if sometimes erratic survival. But Dukas, in giving his gloomy advice, was probably led by the same intention as Ravel when recommending imitation. If a young composer let himself be discouraged by this sort of Toynbee-ish approach to the problems of composition, nothing was lost. If on the other hand he had something to say as a composer, the challenge was going to strengthen his talent.

As for Dukas himself, awareness of the *zeitgeist*'s musical exi-gencies led him not so much to discouragement as to a sort of good-humoured disdain. Unlike Ravel he was not going to allow Stravinsky to influence him – Stravinsky whose position and importance he once defined (1923) with his usual lucidity:

. . . every single one of his works reveals a new and unprecedented Stravinsky. And every single one of his works seems to invent its own rule, which springs from its conception and applies to that work alone. So much so that with Stravinsky the expression confirms the exception.

Such methods Dukas was ready to admire but not to imitate. Yet neither would he repeat himself and add, when there was no charming ballerina to charm, some other competent item to his short catalogue.

The improvisatory ways of the next generation of French musicians went altogether against his grain, and he would never agree to enliven by some broad stroke of the brush the frigidity of academically perfect design. Austrian expressionism, at the other end of the musical map, was outside his scope. Webern, comparable to Dukas for his faultless good taste and for the uncompromising integrity of his musicianship, has, not inappropriately, been called 'the master of triple pianissimo'. Dukas would not conform to such nonconformist *morbidezza*. And there is nothing more respectable than his probably ill-advised decision to prefer a silent composer to a composer of near-silent music.

Dukas

4 The modal province:
Caplet, Kœchlin, Emmanuel

The old mediaeval modes or 'ecclesiastical tones' were resorted to
by Debussy for their static, ornamental, impersonal quality; they
were useful terms, among others, in his anti-romantic vocabulary.
For similar reasons of style and expression, modal patterns are
frequently met with in Ravel's music, and in Dukas's. And among
Debussy's followers three at least settled down in the mediaeval,
plain-chant province; in André Caplet's, Charles Kœchlin's and
Maurice Emmanuel's scores, which have little else in common, the
modal element is essential. So much so that these very remarkable
composers are undeservedly neglected, even in France.

Modality is easily suspect of quaintness. It appears, especially in
Latin countries, to make secular music sound churchy, to introduce
some sort of aural incense into the concert hall – a fragrance whose
facile appeal seems destined to make up, extra-musically, for the
lack of bones and angles and for the intrinsic monotony of a
musical idiom devoid of cadence and modulation.

Yet there are modalists and modalists. And modal mannerisms, so
tiresome in minor composers, cease to be so when merged in the
qualities of a great composer's style.

Caplet

About 1900 at Le Havre the father of a young musician of twenty-
two, then well on his way towards the Prix de Rome, was a frequent
and popular visitor, as the town's best piano-tuner, at the homes of

38

the town's merchant-aristocrats. And among these, Monsieur Maze and his family came to like young André Caplet, his piano playing, his conversation and his romantic good looks, complete with velvet jacket and flowing *lavallière*. To like and to admire and never to forget him: forty years later one of Monsieur Maze's sons, Paul Maze, the Franco-British painter, often told me that in his boyhood Caplet had been the first to acquaint him with the pride and the humility, the humour and the seriousness of 'a man given over to, enwrapt in, and glowing with his art'.

André Caplet's life was marked by many musical, and few other, events. As an accompanist he played the piano, I am told, very much like Benjamin Britten; and by coaching Claire Croiza he made her the greatest of Debussy singers. He became easily the first among the French conductors of his day and was, as such, active in Boston (1910–14); he conducted the premiere of *Le Martyre de Saint Sébastien* (1911) and the first English performance of *Pelléas* (1912).

In the First World War, he was gassed. His lungs never recovered, and he died in his forty-eighth year (1925).

Caplet, of all musicians, had certainly the best opportunity to be influenced by Debussy. They were close friends, and in 1911, time running short for the completing of the music of *Le Martyre de Saint Sébastien*, Debussy entrusted Caplet with part of the scoring – and it has been rumoured that Caplet's collaboration went even further, and that the disciple knew enough about the master's intentions to be able to complete Debussy's score in substance as well as in instrumentation on not a few pages. Small wonder, in consequence, that with Caplet Debussyism has the very unusual aspect of being mere 'Saint-Sebastianism'. Critics and other chroniclers of French music are wont to tell us, in slightly patronizing tones, about Debussy's 'devastating influence' on his friend – the implications being that Caplet lacked originality – but they overlook the strange fact that, with the sole exception of Stravinsky (*Le Roi des Etoiles*, 1912), no other early Debussyist ever dreamt of modelling his music's style on *Le Martyre's*.

There was no trace of impressionism in Caplet's music, and his very singular way of being a Debussy follower was by no means his only originality. Most unlike pagan Debussy, Caplet was primarily a composer of spiritual music. And, unlike even the French religious composers of the romantic era, he chose to belong not to the

D

German (implicitly Protestant) but to the Roman Catholic, mediaeval, Gregorian tradition. His music is meant, not to express or symbolize a dialogue between the Soul and God, but to accompany and adorn a ritual or a sacred narrative. It is certainly meant to be endowed with splendour, but a splendour of the sort that befits, not a sermon preached by a prophet or a vision recounted by a mystic, but a thurible or chalice shaped by a master craftsman like Benvenuto Cellini. Caplet's objective, ornamental art derived its modern archaism from Debussy's, but applied it in a musical sphere that never entered Debussy's scope, and where constant recourse to mediaeval modes was fully justified.

On the other hand there is hardly anything in Caplet reminiscent of Debussy's irony and elusiveness. Caplet's scores, like his performances, were always pieces of precise craftsmanship. He published a collection of imaginative and ingenious *solfeggi – The Singer's Daily Bread* as he called them – and, complementary to this sort of exercise, his *Fables de La Fontaine* are studies in musical prosody of charming sophistication. His *Fantastic Tale* (after Edgar Allan Poe) for harp and strings surpasses in originality and brilliance anything ever written for the harp. His semi-spiritual Cello Concerto (*Épiphanie*) is arresting throughout, and its cadenza fascinating: halting and agitated by turns, and from end to end accompanied by regular *pianissimo* drumbeats, as though to give the 'static principle' its due even amidst the impish and restless rather than 'divine' arabesques of a virtuoso piece.

Nothing, however, in Caplet's short catalogue compares with *Le Miroir de Jésus*, a set of mystery canticles for solo mezzo-soprano, a trio of soprano voices (in the role of angelic announcers), harp and strings. In the unpretentiously poetic text (written by André Gide's friend, the novelist and playwright Henri Ghéon) musical images, once more 'Sebastianesque', are musical counterparts of hieratic icons or intimate *Riches Heures*.

Not by chance this score has recently found a champion in Marcel Couraud, a specialist of avantgarde music. For in spite of wide differences of style and idiom, *Le Miroir* should be performed side by side with Stravinsky's *Canticum Sacrum* or his *Sermon, Narrative and Prayer*, which are sacred music of the same brand as Caplet's – gemlike, hard and faultless.

Kœchlin

To proceed from André Caplet to Charles Kœchlin is like leaving a mediaeval craftsman's workshop for a mediaeval astrologer's den.

Going to this den in a remote part of oldest Paris (near the Arènes de Lutèce) you had to ring the bell three or four times before, Noah-bearded and corduroy-clad, Kœchlin appeared, looked at you out of friendly and keen yet dreamy eyes not unlike a spaniel's, bade you sit down in his studio, at one end of a huge table, and then, at the other end, resumed his copying of some orchestral parts, or his fiddling with some nondescript implement (perhaps something to do with amateur photography) without taking the slightest notice of your presence. After a while, turning away for the time being from an activity that always looked as if it could never be dropped but only interrupted, he would start – or rather would seem to continue – talking *de omnibus rebus et quibusdam aliis*: about the anonymous first performance (in 1911) of Ravel's *Valses nobles*, whose author many failed to identify; about how much he agreed with Stravinsky's appreciation of Delibes and other nineteenth-century French composers of ballet music and comic operas; or about Saint-Saëns, who too was quite a good symphonist; or, again, that in musical politics or general politics anti-Wagnerism was doomed, and anti-Communism inadmissible; or how much better certain out-of-the-way chords would sound with one or two of their constituents tuned a *comma* sharp or flat. Then he would turn to his piano (which apart from table, chairs and half a dozen mysterious boxes and parcels, was all the furniture in his room), and would play a page out of his latest fugue or (modal) chorale with a gentle and precise touch and a most expressive underlining of every change of harmony, but usually with little or no regard for tempo, rhythm and metre. And when, after that, you had to leave, Kœchlin would take you to the door with a *grand seigneur's* affability, and on the landing would not let you off before he had given you his opinion and asked for yours concerning a long new series of topics. It took as much time to break away from Kœchlin as, an hour before, it had taken to establish contact with him, Then, abruptly, he would withdraw, with no more thought of bidding goodbye than Noah, when retiring into his ark.

The same mild and endearing eccentricity is displayed in the vast catalogue of his compositions. For no traceable reason he took to writing pieces for hunting horns by the dozen and duos with bassoon. There is indeed no taste for archaizing in his predilection for mediaeval modes: he was himself mediaeval by temperament and idiosyncrasy.

Classical and romantic tonal composers think that modern (*i.e.* non-mediaeval) music should be organized between its beginning and its end by way of development, recapitulation or other temporal contrasts and symmetries. Kœchlin of course knows about all that, but it is alien to his ear and mind. Little does he care whither his music goes; he just lets it be happy for sounding and resounding here and now: such is his personal way of being true to the 'static' principle.

Thus one of his most sumptuous fugues, the orchestral one in F minor, starts in the manner of Bach, but ends with chords in remote harmonies – a daring mixture of styles, which Kœchlin's innocence and candour provide with an unexpected naturalness.

Kœchlin always seemed to be as little in a hurry to complete his work as twelfth-century builders were to complete their cathedrals. A tireless and by no means slow worker he wrote within a few days the prelude to the *Jungle Book Symphony* (after Kipling) – a superb monodic fantasy and superbly scored – but it took him more than a decade (1925-39) to bring out the whole work, though it was his most important composition, and music which, for its vividness, variety, and orchestral splendour, could perfectly well hold its own on the same programme as Debussy's *Jeux* or *Images*.

Complete performances of this work have been scandalously few. Yet Kœchlin's *Bandar-Log* has been recorded on the same disc as Boulez. Rightly so: nothing could stand nearer to the spirit of disrepect and rootlessness of the 'experimenting 1960s' than this piece by Kœchlin (who died aged eighty-three in 1951): a piece of wild polyphonic fancy, which amidst ironical allusions to the *retour au classique*, portrays the monkeys' antics and grimaces and their suspect cleverness by means of twelve-tone motives, which, as everybody knows, have an equally suspect intellectual way of meandering in everlasting tension and unrest through an intemperately well-tempered chromatic jungle.

The Seven Stars Symphony (1933) is a remarkable example of orchestral choreography-without-ballet. Charlie Chaplin, Douglas Fairbanks and five other perhaps not so unforgettable

Hollywood figures of those days are evoked. Forty years later these musical portraits have lost nothing of their freshness and their originality – an originality which more than in anything else resides in their exceptional discontinuous scoring. For, alone among Debussy's immediate successors, Kœchlin treated orchestration in late Debussy's manner: not as a means of adding colour to a pre-established musical delineation but as an essential element of composition.

Such had indeed been, long before Debussy, the method followed by Berlioz and other orchestral innovators. But Debussy's innovation, and in his wake Kœchlin's, consisted in breaking up the orchestral palette and in using tone-values of unprecedented variety – not for the 'impressionist' purpose of substituting a multiplicity of shades for straightforward simple colours, but as an inventory of novel prime constituents of novel musical structures.

It may be surprising that Kœchlin, a mediaeval and modal designer of chorales, fugues and other studies in unruffled contrapuntal lines, should have also been a builder of sophisticated tone-pavilions, and should have let himself be extra-musically inspired in two of his major works. Yet the spirit of meditation and the spirit of extravaganza have long been perfectly compatible and perhaps complementary, as the whole range of freakish or nightmarish figures prove, carved in stone, in the recesses of almost every Romanesque chapel.

Opera and Mass excepted, every genre of music is represented in Kœchlin's list of more than 220 items. But all-out Kœchlin concerts, as they have been tentatively proposed in France and in England, cannot but be puzzling, for his *œuvre*, it must be admitted, is most unequal. Next to works that are compelling and moving – some very long like *La vieille maison de campagne* (an astonishing set of baroque piano pieces), some very short like his *Chorale on the Name of Fauré* – next to these works there are others such as could have been written by many a nondescript composer of good taste.

Kœchlin himself was (regrettably or happily) unaware of such differences. Mediaeval once more, his outlook was the German mystic's *'der alles gliche schaezet'* – 'who giveth equal value to all things'. High voltage or low voltage, *Carmen* or some very dull comic opera of Gounod's, he was unwilling to discard any work of competent craftsmanship – a frame of mind that made him an

43

excellent teacher and a singularly unprejudiced one. And he was a writer of excellent treatises, most valuable for all craftsmen who want to get away from academic doctrine and routine.

True to type, Kœchlin the teacher cared no less for beginners than for his most advanced pupils. He published a collection of sixty very attractive two-part inventions designed, not unlike Bach's, for turning young pianists into young polyphonists. And in the twenties two already successful young composers, Auric and Sauguet, were among Kœchlin's disciples, as was Desormière, the conductor of the Diaghilev ballet and the first to perform the orchestral music of Boulez two decades later. It was, therefore, not unnatural that Kœchlin, who himself at the turn of the century had been a brilliant pupil in Massenet's, Fauré's and Gedalge's classes, should apply for a professorship at the Paris Conservatoire.

Kœchlin's application was rejected, and only one member of the Conseil Supérieur disagreed with his colleagues, mostly academicians and other figureheads of musical officialdom. The lonely dissenter was Paul Dukas.

Emmanuel

With the last (and oldest) of our three modalists the reference was partly to mediaeval and partly to Greek modes – the latter reference being imaginary rather than substantial, since the only defensible attitude toward the music of ancient Greece is the Socratic attitude: we know that we know nothing about it, or next to nothing.

But Maurice Emmanuel (1862–1938), once Debussy's schoolfellow at the Conservatoire, brought up as both a musician and a scholar, was both ingenious and ingenuous: he ignored controversial and unrewarding sources (like the famous notation of an Apollo hymn) and approached the problem of Greek rhythm from the side of Greek poetry and Greek art. He was probably the first since J. A. le Baïf (not a professional musician, 1532–89) to transliterate the conventional signs of poetic metre ($- \smile \smile$, $- -$, etc) in terms of minims and crochets with the purpose of casting musical metre in the mould of that highly flexible and complex versification in which Aeschylus and Sophocles chose to cast the rhythms of tragedy. At the same time Emmanuel started studying – in France, Greece and Germany – copies of Greek pottery or friezes showing dancers dancing to the accompaniment of a lyre, or an aulos or two. He thought that a musician, aware of the analogies between musical and visual rhythm, would be able to derive from the deceptive immobility of the dancers the style of Greek dancing, as a graphologist is able to derive a writer's gestures and rhythmic impulses from his script.

Moreover, to equip himself with exact notions about dancers' technique the young Emmanuel entered the ballet school of the Paris Opéra; and the results of his dual experience of hieratic urns and choreographic turns were laid down in his much valued thesis *L'Orchestique Grecque* ('*Greek choreography*') which earned him a doctorate from the Sorbonne in 1896.

Dionysian Nietzsche would certainly have liked the idea of a dancing philologist. But for his friends and his pupils, who knew their Emmanuel thirty years later, there is something touchingly ludicrous about imagining him in a Degas scene, among *ballérines*. By now Maurice Emmanuel, a slow-spoken gentleman, was of a decidedly non-balletic aspect. He looked like the clerical choir-master he had been for some years at Sainte Clotilde and also like a huge, untypically stiff and angularly moving tomcat with watchful round eyes and bristling whiskers. And, just as Puss never condones a rebuke, let alone an undeserved one, Maurice Emmanuel, a professor of the History of Music at the Paris Conservatoire, was by 1920 still quite indignant about his dismissal in the eighties from Delibes's composition class because, in a string quartet which he submitted, he had refused to alter a modal key signature into an orthodox tonal one.

If he remained indignant, it was because in his mind and his heart he respected the Establishment's 'tables of value'. He collected the enchanting traditional songs of his native Burgundy, and would readily have provided them – nineteenth century fashion and to please every academic mugwump – with lopsided harmonizations in the conventional major and minor keys. But there was no escape from the legitimate style of their tunes nor from his own uncompromising musicality: he published them with splendid modal accompaniments, laid out not in chords, but in an always apposite and delightfully transparent polyphonic framework.

In contrast with Kœchlin's, Emmanuel's music does not in the least recall its composer's aspect and gait: it is rapid more often than leisurely, always remarkably light, not in expressive content

45

but in texture. Debussy reacted against the romantic malady of over-development ('the laboratory of the void') by suppressing development altogether. Emmanuel's different cure was to thin it out until it became an allusion, and to compress it into the brevity of an aphorism. *Sonatine* III with the theme of a *chanson bourguignonne* fast flitting by; *Sonatine* IV with its twilight-coloured opening, its near-tragic slow movement and its Lisztian and Busoniesque finale, was written for Busoni and employs modes borrowed from Hindu music – in fact, mediaeval modes with an interval or two chromatically altered; *Sonatine* V, orchestrated later, evokes, like Ravel's *Tombeau de Couperin*, eighteenth century dances, but in much less classical, much more distortingly perverse a manner; the dazzling *Sonatine* VI, with very unexpected evocations of Schumann's 'bird as a prophet' and of Italian comic opera – I know of no other example of a set of brilliant, if very difficult, keyboard pieces invented and written by a composer himself unable to play the easiest of Czerny's exercises.

It must be admitted that these *Sonatines* have hitherto had both their difficulty and their brevity against them. Their unusual virtuosity discourages many a virtuoso; and many listeners are too slow in focusing their attention not to miss the music's points of interest and beauty. Today it may perhaps be hoped that listening to Webern many have counteracted such lazy habits.

In 1926 Emmanuel re-entered the Paris Opéra, this time not the ballet school but the stage, the tiers and the pit, yet again under quite unforeseen circumstances. Th. Reinach, a well known Hellenist, was relaxing from studying his texts by amusing himself with a French translation in alexandrines of Aeschylus's *Persians*. Being an academician he had little difficulty in finding a company ready to bring out his *chef d'œuvre*, and he asked Emmanuel, whom he knew as the author of *L'Orchestique Grecque* and a music drama after Aeschylus's *Prometheus*, to provide the *Persians* with incidental music. Emmanuel set to work, and before long Reinach's drama shrank to the size of a libretto while Emmanuel's intended stage-music expanded into a full-fledged opera. Very reasonably Reinach agreed to this change of proportion and purpose, and had *Salamine* accepted at the Opéra.

Not a few musicians were delighted. Dukas – always Dukas – wrote to Emmanuel exactly the letter his music deserved. But it stands to reason that with the rank and file of opera-goers, an hieratic opera like *Salamine* (an opera without a love scene and with its dramatic climax – the actual battle of Salamis – merely figuring as an off-stage event, in a messenger's narrative) could hardly hope for more than the *succès d'estime* it obtained. Extreme conciseness is uncongenial – even more than to concert-goers – to opera audiences, who instinctively want to be cradled in an opera's musical events as in comfortable rocking chairs. Moreover with *Salamine* listeners as well as performers could not but feel disconcerted by a musical language which displays a great diversity of unusual rhythmical patterns derived from the metres of Greek tragic poetry as well as a great diversity of harmonic and polyphonic patterns, purporting to be derived from Greek modes, but in fact born of a most original composer's imagination and creative power.

Yet *Salamine*, that concert-goers' opera, is by no means operatically ineffective. The main scenes are not only magnificent music, but also, once more in the static and ornamental style, impressive drama, a tragedy of pride and humiliation, of Hubris and Nemesis. It is tempting to compare *Salamine* with another great score *da rappresentazione,* Stravinsky's *Oedipus Rex,* written about the same time. Both composers have accepted the modern dialogue with the past. Stravinsky refers to seventeenth- and eighteenth-century style, Emmanuel to much older traditions; Stravinsky's antique decor resembles that of de Chirico's statues and Doric columns, ironically introduced in modern surroundings. Maurice Emmanuel's dealings with *Tyche* and *Heimarmene* recall Thomas Hardy's and Paul Valéry's.

During Emmanuel's lifetime the scholar's and musicologist's authority overshadowed the composer's. His phrase 'le tyran Ut' became the warcry of every musician who, as a composer, practised or, as a performer, favoured the modal style. Today his commentary on *Pelléas* is still one of the best things written about Debussy. His vast *Histoire de la langue musicale* is far from indifferent, but over-furnished with erudite detail – most unlike his music, which awaits patiently and can afford to await confidently the day of rediscovery. A composer's novelty of language is not an unforgiveable sin. It escapes the Bottomless Pit, though it may have to endure Purgatory.

5 Two composers react against Debussy: Schmitt and Roussel

Unworkable reaction: Florent Schmitt

To be uncommonly gifted as a composer is one thing; to be a great composer quite another. Florent Schmitt (1870–1958) was certainly gifted as gifted can be, and technically a master never caught napping. His adroitness in linking chord with chord, phrase with phrase and in spinning out long stretches of musical discourse was uncanny. His orchestration is so competent that any score of his is a bad conductor's paradise: let every instrumentalist just play what is written, and every detail of a rich orchestral fabric will automatically fall into place.

Neither are good taste and elegance wanting, but this never-failing elegance is one of the signs of what is amiss with Florent Schmitt: it is not nobility of character but lack of character that keeps vulgarity from his music. Simple or involved and (in his later works) much more often involved than simple, his musical ideas are second-hand and commonplace. Every composer hitherto dealt with in this essay has, as the Bellman would say, his 'unmistakable marks'. You hear ten bars of D'Indy's, of Ravel's, and you exclaim: 'This is D'Indy; this is Ravel, or the Devil!' With Florent Schmitt the alternative is not the Devil but some hybrid won from Debussy and Franck, Fauré and Liszt, or Wagner and Rimsky-Korsakov.

His Psalm XLVI came out in 1906. At its second performance, probably the first adequate one, in 1910, it met with a triumphal reception. It was described as 'titanic' and 'cyclopean', and up-to-date chroniclers marvelled that, so few years after *Pelléas*, that masterwork of delicacy, modern French music 'had been rescued from an impasse' by the emergence of a complementary masterwork of vigour. But, in modern disguise, it meant a downright reaction against everything Debussy stood for: a return to good old post-romantic rhetoric and pomposity. Psalm XLVI's pretended grandeur is not even the grandeur of the 'colossus with feet of clay'. It is clay all over – hollow yet plethoric. So much so that a story went around that Schmitt, noticing during a rehearsal that the double-basses were pausing for a few bars, came up and produced a pencil: 'Wait a minute, I'll give you something to do . . .' A dubious story, but typical enough to be at least *ben trovato*.

Between 1910 and 1960 Florent Schmitt's undeniable prestige among French composers was hardly ever challenged: an exemplary case of successful pseudo-modernism. After all he used a harmonic and melodic vocabulary that was 'advanced' and unafraid of dissonance. At the tumultuous first night of *The Rite of Spring* he apostrophized a party of hissing society ladies: 'Shut up, you tarts from the sixteenth!' (The sixteenth arrondissement is the Paris Kensington.) Conservative critics disparaged him. On the other hand those who liked Debussy and Ravel liked Florent Schmitt too at first. And some time was to pass before it appeared that his scores had little in common with Debussy's or Ravel's except a few 'impressionist' mannerisms; and that his complacent, lush, opulent aesthetic had much in common with the style of the Pont Alexandre, a late nineteenth century bridge in Paris, and of Edwardian Regent Street. It was, therefore, quite apposite that the Academy was very reluctant to award him the Prix de Rome in 1900, but in 1936 only too glad to elect him – and turn down another candidate, Stravinsky, then a French citizen.

Florent Schmitt's looks were unofficial, his behaviour conveniently and pleasantly anti-conformist. A native from Blamont, near the German border, he liked being called 'the Wild-boar from the Ardennes'. Yet his manners were frank and outspoken rather than aggressive, his retorts witty, and often on a par with those of an Aldous Huxley heroine who, when South America was mentioned, would remark that it reminded her of a leg of mutton. As a music critic in one of the important papers, *Le Temps*, he always had a well-tuned compliment ready for a composing belle, or a performing one, and was generally, though not always, benevolent when reviewing his male colleagues' work.

Among his works, a list which goes up to Op. 130, orchestral music is represented by ballets and symphonic poems like *La Tragédie de Salomé* – a genteel Salomé, owing a lot to Debussy, Dukas and Rimsky, but hardly preferable to Strauss's plebeian and original one – and chamber-music works, vocal or instrumental, none of them better, none worse, than his Sonata for violin and piano: compositions made up of odds and ends – brilliant odds and sentimental ends – technically coherent, if diffuse, but strangely unsatisfactory works of luxuriant and garrulous musical materialism.

Yet it would be unjust not to add that in two works at least – works dedicated to the memory of two musicians he loved and admired – a different, much more sensitive and human Florent Schmitt appears. And I think that *Cippus feralis* (for orchestra) and *Stèle* (for piano), written in homage to Fauré and Dukas, should be saved from the oblivion into which, since his death in 1958, this imperfect master's music is falling.

Workable reaction: Roussel

An early commentator of Roussel's, Paul Landormy, defined him as 'Un Debussy ayant le sens du contrepoint'. Not a bad definition, especially if we improve it into 'A rebellious Debussy follower who made counterpoint the charter of his independence'.

Roussel would not accept Debussy's 'static principle'. Rather than juxtapose chords, he would superpose motives. And the intrinsic mobility of these motives could not but turn him into a composer of long drawn-out developments, and thereby into a restorer of sonata form and symphony. Yet none but a Debussy follower could ever have symphonized or sonatized in Roussel's manner. His style, most unlike Florent Schmitt's, never paid the slightest tribute to the rhetoric of post-romanticism. His *sinfonia* never dreamt of being either *eroica* or *domestica*, never aimed at portraying its composer as an angry young man or a metaphysician. Vocal or instrumental, symphonic or *da camera*, his works are without exception musical entertainments, impersonal in expression, unmistakably personal in the material employed and method of employing it: always those long, widespread, meandering lines, made of disjoined melodic elements, set against similar and independent lines, all of them flexible, yet most of them angular. Lines that combine into scintillating metallic textures of singular transparency and lightness – of so weightless a quality, indeed, that the nethermost line feels ill at ease as the bass. Against every grain of scholastic habit this bass line of Roussel's, determined to be just as free and mobile as the treble line, refuses to have the basic, balancing and settling functions of dominant or tonic in its care. Small wonder if Roussel, like Berlioz, has been taxed with being unwilling or unable to know right bass from wrong bass. There is, indeed, something unsettled and floating about Roussel's musical structures. His unsentimental, non-psychological melodic design resembles the non-representational patterns of oriental carpets. And in his polyphony, which so adventurously flouts the law of tonal gravitation, there is something of the magic and the delight of flying carpets.

Born (1869) in Tourcoing in French Flanders, Albert Roussel liked to affirm his Flemishness. Yet this chauvinist Fleming looked as if, not Rubens or Jordaens, but El Greco or Zurbarán had painted his portrait, or even Delacroix during his stay in North Africa. Dark, slim and wiry, one imagined him on horseback in turban and burnouse and solitary in the desert, rather than feasting among hosts of red cheeks and joyous bellies at a *kermesse*. Nothing boisterous about him and no easy familiarity : courteous and unassuming, Roussel seemed always a little distant, as though half-absorbed by his meditations. But generous and hospitable, and loyal to a friend or guest, as becomes an aristocratic bedouin.

An orphan at the age of eight, he stayed first with his grandfather, the burgomaster of Tourcoing, who played the viola, and then with an aunt, who provided him with his first music teacher, a spinster organist who doted on her young pupil's playing the piano not only 'par cœur' but even 'avec sentiment'. Yet in his provincial surroundings he had very little occasion to feed his musical curiosity on anything but a few transcriptions of operatic airs *à la mode* And, fascinated by the sea (only some thirty miles distant) and by Jules Verne's tales of adventure and navigation he soon disbanded the imaginary orchestra he used to conduct in his uncle's garden and took command of an imaginary yet tangible ship, figured by a prow of chairs and a poop of armchairs in his uncle's parlour.

Between 1884 and 1887 in Paris he prepared for his admission to the École Navale. At the same time he resumed his piano lessons and before long his musical experience included some Mozart and Beethoven. In 1887 he entered the Navy, and boarded an old school-ship anchored in Brest harbour. His accomplishments as a musician were made use of every Sunday morning, when Mass was celebrated on deck. And on one occasion he asserted himself as a musician for whom music is music, independent of context: no better score being available, he turned the march from Offenbach's *La Belle Hélène* into quite acceptable church-music by slowing down its tempo. On the other hand Roussel proved quite an acceptable sailor. Navigating on several other men-of-war, he was soon promoted. Nevertheless he resigned his commission in 1894. He had already started composing, encouraged by Julien Koszul (an organist again), head of the Roubaix Conservatoire. Then, one of his friends, himself a sailor, back from leave in Paris, (mendaciously) told him that Colonne the famous conductor, after being shown a score of Roussel's, had declared that its composer should not hesitate to quit the Navy and follow his musical vocation. And this apocryphal verdict matched the promptings of his own *daimonion* too well not to be decisive.

Again in Paris he took lessons in harmony, counterpoint and fugue-writing, with Eugène Gigout – the third organist to come Roussel's way – who threw him headlong into the universe of Bach, Handel, Mozart and Beethoven, and declared 'that his pupil's gift for fugue-writing amounts to genius'. A little later, he entered the recently founded Schola Cantorum, and let himself be initiated to composition, scoring and history of music by Vincent D'Indy, whose sense of symphonic architecture was meeting Roussel's taste and instinct more than halfway, but whose Wagnerian dogmas left him wholly unimpressed. For Roussel, fugue-writing pupil of three organists and one dogmatist, was to be the disciple of one musician – Debussy, who never cared for the organ, never published a fugue, and was anti-dogmaticism personified.

In an early chamber-music work, *Divertissement* for piano, woodwind and horn (Op. 6, 1906), Roussel's originality is apparent and his later personal style foreshadowed; other early works, such as his much-played Piano Suite (Op. 14, 1910), show D'Indy's influence, and display Roussel's solidity of make not yet combined with his later gossamer touch. Nevertheless the first group of more ambitious scores is Debussy-begotten through and through, for its impressionism, exoticism and atmospheric sensuousness. Such are his First Symphony called *Le Poème de la Forêt* (Op. 7, 1904–6), *Suite symphonique* for chamber orchestra (Op. 13), and *Évocations*, choral and orchestral, (Op. 15, 1910–11) written after, and under the spell of, Monsieur and the young Madame Roussel's passage to India. In 1912 his ballet *Le Festin de l'Araignée*, a Midsummer Night's Dreamish affair, still echoes Debussy and harks back to the hardly less modern and certainly not less Shakespearian Berlioz.

With Op. 18, the opera-ballet *Padmavâti*, we find Roussel well on his way towards independence. India-inspired again, it is the tragedy of a rajah who, lest his city be annihilated to the last inhabitant, agrees to surrender Padmavâti, his queen, to his conqueror. He escapes from this sacrilegious dilemma : Padmavâti kills him and, an irreproachable suttee, joins him on his pyre.

Roussel's score is magnificent: choral and orchestral masses, and Augmented 2nds and Diminished 3rds, and every element of oriental melody, harmony and colour, are handled with consummate and tranquil mastery. The music that tells this story of heroic weakness and heroic determination is the more impressive for telling it with that unsentimental aloofness incumbent on followers of Debussy as well as followers of the Brahmins.

The breakthrough in Roussel's evolution, however, occurs with Op. 22 and 23, the short symphonic poem *Pour une Fête de Printemps* (1920), and the Second Symphony in B flat (1919–20) – an intentional and long-meditated breakthrough: 'For several years,' Roussel wrote much later, 'I have reflected upon my art. . . . I had been captivated by impressionism, and my music was linked, too much perhaps, with extrinsic elements and a technique of picturesqueness, which – I discovered later on – was detrimental to its specific truth. I resolved, therefore, to endow my harmonies with a wider scope, and get nearer to the idea of a music intended and constructed to be self-sufficient.'

Colour recedes, geometry comes to the fore, and the mature Roussel's disencumbered polyphony, which takes unresolved dissonance in its stride, aims at satisfying its listener's sense of musical logic rather than flattering his taste for musical charm.

To encourage the first listeners of his 'difficult' Second Symphony – perhaps the best, if the most austere, of the four – he added a 'programme' – perhaps a belated homage to D'Indy's aesthetics – and later on confessed that such a programme was 'contrary to that symphony's spirit'. And – programme or no programme – this score, whose harshness (real or assumed) was oddly enough attributed to Stravinsky's influence, had the honour of being ill received by that ever-grumbling set of musical epicures who had also disapproved of Debussy's and Fauré's later works.

By then Roussel had found his style and his way. His entire *œuvre* comprises sixty works. It took him two decades (1898–1918) to produce the first twenty, another two decades to add the remaining forty, and these as notable for unity of manner as for diversity of matter.

This assuredness of form, this pre-ordainedness of musical procedure entailed no small musical risks; and, in fact, with some of his most successful works – the Third Symphony, the ballet *Bacchus et Ariane*, the *Suite en Fa* (a showpiece of *Retour à Bach*) – original though they are (and perhaps even *because* they are so strongly and systematically hallmarked), not a few convinced Rousselites feel uneasy. At a moment when every other worthwhile composer was tight-rope walking between the devil of barren artificiality and the deep sea of defunct convention, the gods grew jealous of Roussel who dared to write with an eighteenth century musician's straightforwardness and brisk saltatory naïvety and with a pre-Beethoven disregard for the tragic antinomies that assail the makers of modern music. Weightlessness, we have said, adds magic to Roussel's polyphonic carpets. But now and then Roussel, yielding to an excess of confidence and simplification, seems to suspend his music in thin air and to dilute its magic in some sort of private academicism, an academicism no less academic for deriving its formula not from general conventions but from personal inventions. Flying carpets lose a good deal of their spell when it looks as if they were scheduled to leave Le Bourget airfield every Tuesday.

But even so, Roussel's talent had a way with it that placated the gods more than once. His Psalm LXXX, written to the words of the English Bible, is as grand a sacred score as was ever composed by an agnostic. His Piano Concerto, not a virtuoso's favourite, is entrancing chamber-orchestral music *con cembalo concertato* with one of the finest slow movements imagined by a musician of our time. And his Second Violin Sonata, his Trio for strings, and a lied like *Jazz dans la nuit* are among the scores wherein a great composer's alchemy has turned counterpoint and geometry into musical essence 'burning bright'.

Two composers react against Debussy

In 1914, Roussel wrote to his wife: 'It's facing the sea that we shall let our lives be drawn toward their conclusion, and in our last sleep we shall still be listening to the sea's distant murmur....'

In 1937 he was buried, a stone's throw from his house, in the cimetière marin of Varengeville, near Dieppe. And, as atlantic rhythms come and go – abrupt and irregular, and resembling those so often met with in Roussel's scores – his tomb is visited by sun and storm.

Roussel

6 Renaissance of Spanish music: Albéniz, Granados, De Falla

Spanish music had been dormant for centuries. The memory of Encina, Victoria, Cabezón, Morales had faded (to be revived much later through recording and broadcasting). In the eighteenth century when folklore was habitually ignored by serious composers, one of them, a great musician and a Spaniard by adoption, had listened to and let himself occasionally be inspired by popular music as practised in Spanish town and country: Domenico Scarlatti, who thereby was to induce Albéniz and Granados (as pianists) to perform Scarlatti sonatas, and De Falla (as a composer) to choose Scarlatti as a master of style and expression.

But, no more than Bach revivals suffice to foster new classic composers, would reference to Scarlatti have by itself produced a new Spanish school. It was a sidetrack in the evolution of music, the path followed by romantics eager for the picturesque, that, as an aftermath of romanticism, led Spanish musicians to 'hispanicizing', as it made other composers elsewhere turn nationalists and folklorists when staying at home or, when going abroad, exoticists and explorers after 'local colour'.

Such is, as regards hispanicism, the *raison d'être*, and the role (not an important one) of Glinka's *Jota Aragonesa*, Schumann's *Spanisches Liederspiel*, or Chopin's *Bolero*; and later on, during the Indian summer of globe-trotting romanticism, the role of similar pieces by Tchaikowsky or Rimsky-Korsakov. (Hugo Wolf's *Spanisches Liederbuch* deals with the musical spirit of a country called Spain by its inventor, and to be found nowhere but in the composer's imagination.) *Carmen*, on the other hand, and *España*, rarely accepted by Spanish ears as dyed in the wool, are nevertheless genuine – from the French point of view: influenced by good French literature about Spain (Mérimée, Gautier) and by perhaps not so good Spanish melodies sung in Paris drawing rooms – perhaps not so good in themselves, but perfectly serviceable models for Bizet's and Chabrier's excellent ones. With Debussy at the very time of the incipient renaissance of Spanish music it was going to be give-and-take: Debussy would listen to Spain; Spain would listen to *Iberia*, *La Puerta del Vino*, and *Soirée dans Grenade*. And Ravel had his Spanish aspect by right of birth.

Traditional melodies and rhythms were, in Spain and elsewhere, within easy reach of composers in quest of creating a new and vernacular kind of music. But in Spain alone folklore happened to have already been shaped into professional composers' scores: dozens of musical comedies, called *tonadillas* and *zarzuelas*, had been written in this style between 1860 and 1890 and with great popular success. These operettas are – one of the oddities of the state of music in nineteenth century Spain – fascinating glossaries of Spanish musical idiom. For the 'zarzuelists' did not just take vernacular elements in their stride. They were by no means naïve improvisers; they knew their mind and their purpose, and were well educated. One of the most successful among them, Francisco Asenjo Barbieri (1823-94), an author of seventy-seven *zarzuelas*, was also a learned editor of fifteenth-century vocal music (*cancioneros*). And twentieth-century Spanish music is no less indebted to Barbieri – to the zarzuelist as well as to the musicologist – than to Felipe Pedrell (1841-1922), that other musicologist (and teacher), who is much oftener mentioned, because Albéniz, Granados, and De Falla attended, each for a short time, his composition class in Barcelona.

Albéniz

There is something oddly elusive about Isaac Albéniz's life and work. He was born (1860) in the charming village of Camprodón in the Catalan Pyrenees not far from the French border, and we know that before writing his genuinely Spanish *Iberia* (composed at the end of his life), he wrote, at dates impossible to ascertain, a good deal of indifferent piano music in the post-romantic manner. We know him to have been a virtuoso of almost Lisztian stature; we know little about his education as a pianist, except that he began as a child prodigy and was Marmontel's pupil in Paris and Brassin's in Brussels. We know he met Liszt in Weimar, but know nothing else about their meeting. We know that besides Pedrell in Barcelona, academic Jadassohn, erudite Gevaert and doctrinarian D'Indy were his teachers in Leipzig, Brussels and Paris; but we know nothing about these several professors' influence on him, and may suspect that Albéniz the pianist was the only efficient master of Albéniz the composer. We know that he started travelling at the age of ten: first all through Spain; then to America, taking in on his way music of the sort that never passes the threshold of any self-respecting music school; that he played dance music in sailors' bars, and later on performed Couperin, Bach, Scarlatti, Beethoven and Chopin in fashionable drawing rooms and concert halls. We do not know how that young buccaneer of the keyboard came to be commissioned by an English theatre-loving banker to set his (the banker's) libretti to music. Two heavy-weight and downright nineteenth-century music dramas were the result, followed in 1896 by a comic opera, *Pepita Jiménez*, which stands near to the *zarzuela* tradition.

Meanwhile Albéniz's piano writing advanced by degrees – *Chants d'Espagne, Suites espagnoles, La Vega* – towards *Iberia*, his main achievement. *Iberia*, comprising a dozen pieces, is a *chef-d'œuvre* of decorative polyphony: made of every Iberian sort of ornament – florid arabesques, in the sense of the word's etymology; Andalusian rhythms; melodic recitatives declaimed *alla Castillana* or *alla Cubana*. It is perhaps to this concourse of different styles, rather in the taste and manner of 'colonial baroque', or else to Scarlatti's influence, that Albéniz as a harmonist owes his predilection for clashing acciaccaturas – those imperious dissonant accents, which form so unexpected and so welcome a contrast with the other elements of a musical discourse remarkable for its complacent lack of distinction.

This music's character and rank are also elusive. Meretricious virtuosity – or a sudden sumptuous welling up of hitherto unexplored energies of the Spanish musical genius? Let us quote Debussy: 'Never has music attained such a diversity of impressions and colours : dazzled by a torrent of images, we have to close our eyes. . . .'

Having dazzled Debussy and befriended Fauré and Dukas, Albéniz died (1909) in Cambo, a spa not far from Ravel's birthplace, on the French side of the Pyrenees.

Granados

'I'm not a musician, I'm an artist,' confessed Granados: a most un-Albéniz confession – fortunately for Albéniz. . . .

Enrique Granados, that 'little Spanish Grieg' (as Roland-Manuel defined him) born in Lérida (1867), was a nicely educated and refined bourgeois with an amateur's gift for painting and a superior aptitude for writing music. Resembling Albéniz in one respect, he was an outstanding pianist, but the path of his life ran as smoothly as Albéniz's was rough and adventurous. Only his and his wife's deaths were dramatic: they went down with the liner *Sussex*, a victim of Germany's submarine warfare in 1916.

Granados the composer began to be spoken of and performed after he brought out his first set of *Danzas Españolas* in 1892: well-tempered images of Spanish rhythm – pleasant and quite reassuring to listen to after a look at Goya's frightening evocations of Spanish dancing and gestures.

Strangely enough Granados adored Goya, felt overwhelmed by him, and proclaimed that he wanted to be nothing but the translator into music of Goya's inspiration 'which so perfectly expressed the people of Spain in every act and at every moment'. Yet in Granados's music one would look in vain for anything evoking the *Dos de Mayo* or the *Caprichos*. If Goya is at all present in the *Goyescas* for piano and in the *Tonadillas* for voice and piano, it is the Goya of the meekest of his early tapestries. Moreover this innocent late eighteenth-century Goya was translated by Granados into still more innocent, half-impressionist, half-Mendelssohnian post- nineteenth-century music. However, these piano pieces were technically exacting and rewarding, and much performed between 1910 and 1940. But when Granados tried to build up his *Goyescas* to the size of a stagework, even the pale but genuine Spanish colours that distinguished his piano writing were lost in the regrettably Pucciniesque make-up of his opera score.

De Falla

Albéniz was a Catalan by birth and an Andalusian by ear and

heart. Andalusian Manuel De Falla felt and wrote like a Castilian. And for him Latin America – the land of adolescent's dreams and man's adventure to Albéniz – was to be an exile's refuge. Yet, dissimilar though they were, when Albéniz died in France, there was to succeed him none but De Falla, who had just written the one Albéniz-type score he was ever to write, his *Quatre Pièces espagnoles* for piano. This was his first Spanish work: *La Vida Breve* (1905) had been his tribute to both Wagnerism and verismo.

In contrast to Albéniz, De Falla was neither particularly attracted by nor quite at ease with the piano: and his one popular piece is a transcription (*Danza rituel del Fuego* from *El Amor Brujo*). His *Fantasia bética* (1919) is a rather formless succession of arresting details: written when De Falla was looking for new patterns and another palette, it falls between two styles. And the quality of his very beautiful and moving *Homenaje* to Dukas (1938) owes nothing to the instrument it happened to be written for. About Albéniz the flamboyant pianist there was always something comfortably and good-naturedly sensual, as a homely snapshot shows: expectation of a nice meal inscribed in his bearded smile. Nothing flamboyant about grave, clean-shaven, eremitical De Falla, all skin and bones, the incarnation (with as little flesh as possible) of asceticism. Albéniz seems never to have doubted or hesitated, and his best and most personal music came as naturally as the rest of his output. De Falla was always anxiously in search of his true self, and he finally embarked on his unfinished last enterprise as one entering an inscrutable and inescapable labyrinth.

How strange and how admirable that De Falla's chronic hesitancy and his humble readiness to accept other composers' ascendancy and influence should each time have resulted in a work of fascinating originality – every single one of his few scores being the most ingenious solution of a problem that a modern musician in quest of his style and his techniques had been intent on solving for many a month.

Born (1876) in Cádiz, about 1900 he studied composition with Pedrell. Awarded the Real Academia's prize for *La Vida Breve*, in 1905, he made for Paris in 1907, where Debussy was the first musician he went to see: 'Maître, I'm so happy to meet you – I love French music!'

It was not one of Debussy's good days, and for once shelving urbanity and even patriotism: 'You love French music? Well, I don't. Goodbye, Monsieur.' But De Falla was to come back before long, under Paul Dukas's wing, and the relation became as cordial as could be expected from distant Debussy and shy De Falla – who (almost like the hero of a fairy tale) had planned a short visit to Paris, then stayed for seven years. His recent compositions (the *Pièces espagnoles* among them) were published by Durand, and it was in Paris that he wrote the *Siete Canciones Españolas*: strictly authentic melodies to very unconventional settings, perfect in character.

After these *Siete Canciones* no original folklore melody ever reappeared in any of De Falla's scores. He distrusted popular tradition, and suspected the pure *cante jondo* to have, more often than not, been gypsified – turned into flamenco. Bartók's curiosity and passion for ethnologist's fieldwork – for collecting, recording and sifting traditional music – was quite alien to his temperament, but like Bartók he had an infallible gift for inventing music made of the same stuff as the truest popular chant. Musicologists have tried hard to trace his sources. In vain: for there was no other source than his native Spanishness – the nothing but Spanishness of his musician's instinct which made for the glamour, the imaginary folklore and the immediate success of the three works he wrote before 1920 : the *Noches en los Jardines de España* (1909-15), *El Amor Brujo* (1915), and *El Sombrero de Tres Picos* (1919). These works are much more ingenuously Spanish than his later ones, in spite of obvious French influence: Debussy pervades the *Nights*; to Dukas the two ballets' scoring owes more than a few of its sparks.

The *España Gitana* of *El Amor Brujo* differs widely from the eighteenth century Spain depicted in *The Three-cornered Hat*, that perfect translation into music – how much better than that by Granados! – of Goya's images. Scarlatti, too, has his part in this eighteenth-century evocation. Scarlattian mannerisms are alluded to and stylized; and – to suit the sinewy dryness of motive and rhythm – even the scoring now and then renounces luxuriance.

This manner of 'slim' scoring is one of the marks of De Falla's ultimate style. The ascetic composer scorns charm and picturesqueness. The heritage of folklore is, if not altogether rejected, at least thinned out: only the ghost of folklore – maybe a powerful ghost – is allowed to move about in this quintessential and damn-the-tourists sort of Spanish music. As to French influence De Falla seems determined to go beyond at least one of Debussy's exigencies: where Monsieur Croche would only accept 'music's bare flesh', his Spanish disciple goes straight for flayed music's nerve and bone. And Scarlatti's pert acciaccaturas are hardened into grim dissonances resulting from polytonal counterpoint.

As though to keep his distance from anything to do with realism and to gratify his taste for puppet shows – that most unrealistic form of play – he chose for his next work the episode of *El Retablo de Maese Pedro* in *Don Quixote*. (And, with De Falla, Don Quixote's intervention in the puppet's strife seems to prolong Cervantes's satirical purpose by satirizing any veristic approach.) The characters express themselves in a speedy recitative – of the most *secco* variety – and the instrumental design, be it accompaniment or interlude, seems to owe nothing to brush or pencil, but to be drawn with the driest of dry-points.

The harpsichord, in those days (1923) still a rare guest, has quite an important role in *El Retablo*'s strange scoring. And in 1926 De Falla wrote, for Wanda Landowska – who played it once and never again – his Concerto for harpsichord, violin, alto, flute, oboe and clarinet: perhaps his most accomplished score, and a wiry, dissonant, uncompromising one. The magician of *El Amor Brujo* seems to have retired to a hermit's den, scorched earth all round, inaccessible to all but the few who are meant to be attracted and enchanted by this fiery and austere stylization of Spanish music made up of ragged fiddlers' and pipers' fiddling and piping, plucked strings' metallic expostulations and ecstatic processionists' chant.

The aging De Falla, a solitary hypochondriac, suffered from an ill-defined nervous disease. At his home in Granada his familiars had to shield him from the slightest noise, yet the few visitors admitted to his presence were startled by the ticking of unaccountably numerous clocks – to them irritatingly obtrusive, but unnoticed and even unheard by noise-obsessed Don Manuel.

After his friend García Lorca's death De Falla left Spain for Argentina (1940), never to return. And for seven other years he went on sketching and re-sketching, writing and rewriting, page after page of the score destined to set to music *L'Atlántida,* a hyper-baroque mystery play. Spanish history, Greek mythology and prophetic symbolism had been assembled by Verdaguer, the Catalan poet, into a poem of noble diction, congenial to De Falla the mystic patriot – but, alas, at the same time into a very untidy libretto, most uncongenial to De Falla the neat and almost over-precise musician, and altogether absurd for a composer as scrupu-lously hankering after perfection as Ravel, and as critical and self-critical and disillusioned as Dukas.

After De Falla's death (1947) the Spanish Government commis-sioned the editing (and completing) of the *Atlántida* manuscript. Very few musicians approve of the result, which was released and performed some fifteen years later. Excellent De Falla is, obviously, here and there met with in E. Halffter's score. But on the whole some unfinished novel by Bernanos edited by Pierre Benoît – or, to translate this comparison, E. M. Forster completed by Robert Hichens – would not be much less satisfactory.

To revert to De Falla and conclude: his music, with its novelty – not of language but of accent – has been the first Spanish music never redolent of salon or saloon. Luminous, austere and intense, it owes its luminosity to Spain's pagan heritage, and its intensity and austerity to the heritage of Escorial-minded Spain. But in one respect it differs from almost all great Spanish art: there is nothing reminiscent of cruelty, bullring or *auto-da-fé* in Manuel de Falla's even, civilized and admirably humane music.

Katey 74

De Falla

Interlude I :
A dialogue about Puccini

Pantalone [to the Emperor of China]: We Italians, Your Majesty, always enjoy watching murder and manslaughter on the stage. Rather an atrocious taste, I admit.
Busoni, *Turandot*, Act I, Tableau 2, Scene 3

ADVERSARIUS: . . . and, to begin with, Puccini should not figure at all in this essay: an opera of Puccini's is no more twentieth-century music than a concerto of Tchaikovsky's. Puccini is nineteenth century all over.

ADVOCATUS: That remains to be seen; and dates are dates. Only one half of Puccini's successful works belong to the *ottocento*: *Manon Lescaut* (1893), *La Bohème* (1896) and *Tosca* (1900). His most popular score, *Madame Butterfly*, was written between 1901 and 1904; and the two preferred by connoisseurs are *Gianni Schicchi* (1916) and *Turnadot*, whose composition, started in 1920, was interrupted by the composer's death in 1924.

ADVE: No doubt about all that. But if dates are dates, style is style. And nobody would dream of naming the composer of *Bohème*, famous though he is, alongside the composer of *Pelléas*. Neither would even those who have no particular liking for Richard Strauss mention *Madam Butterfly* and *Salomé* in the same breath.

ADVO: You're quite mistaken, I'm afraid. A few months ago, a work you greatly admire, Busoni's *Doktor Faust*, was recorded. Let me quote from the first lines of the commentary, written by a well

64

known German critic : '... Busoni was the last born of an amazing decade which gave the world a great composer every other year. In 1858 Puccini was born, in 1860 Mahler, in 1862 Debussy, in 1864 Strauss, in 1866 Busoni ...'

ADVE : But doesn't this linking of names make you shudder – and more justifiably so than Nietzsche when hearing about 'Goethe *and* Schiller'?

ADVE : But doesn't this linking of names make you shudder – and originality. His skill and instinct as an *homme de théâtre* among composers can easily compare with Strauss's. Nobody has ever contested that he was one of nature's musicians. And though I admit it proves nothing, it is none the less significant that, alone among his peers, he can boast of a long lineage of creative music-makers. Ever since Giacomo (born 1702) all the Puccinis had been church musicians in Lucca; and so well known even outside *our* Giacomo's native town that when, as a boy of sixteen, he walked for thirty miles to hear another composer's work. ...

ADVE: ... certainly his only performance resembling Bach's ...

ADVO: ... when, I was going to say, too poor to pay for a railway ticket, he walked to Pisa (and back) to hear (and see) *Aïda*, he was sure that a Puccini would never be refused free admittance to the opera house.

ADVE: His heredity certainly favoured his being a musician. His personal inclination made him an operatic one. I don't see anything that made him a twentieth century composer.

ADVO : *I* do. His much decried *verismo*, the most conspicuous mark of his music, is perhaps no more essential in Puccini than impressionism is in Debussy. But at that time this *verismo* was something new. Zola and his followers at once spotted and praised it as a translation into music of dramatic naturalism. Stemming from Verdi's, Puccini's operatic style is altogether different from Verdi's.

ADVE: Most regrettably so.

ADVO: Pray don't swap indictments in the middle of the trial. Do you reproach Puccini with being not modern enough or not traditional enough?

ADVE: Shall I surprise you by saying that it is not so contradictory to charge him with both? Young nineteenth century Puccini wrote *Manon Lescaut*, an opera containing, especially in its first part, quite a number of duos, ensembles, even a madrigal – which, without being Verdi, are pleasant instances of the Italian operatic manner. Later on, and already towards the conclusion of *Manon Lescaut,* he took to *verismo.* This was indeed a new style, but not, as it would have been with a modern composer, a new *musical* style: it was not music renewed, but music reduced. Compare, first, *Rigoletto* and *Traviata* with Victor Hugo's *Le Roi s'amuse* and Dumas's *La Dame aux Camélias,* and then *La Bohème* and *Tosca* with Murger's novel and Sardou's play. The dramatic subject matter is equally unsavoury in every one of these four operas. But Verdi, by means of *bel canto* and all the other operatic devices and inventions, has turned second-rate drama into first-rate music and into wholly self-sufficient music. So much so that, for example, in Liszt's *Rigoletto* Paraphrase it loses nothing for being deprived of text, voice, and stage.

ADVO: Puccini paraphrases, too, have proved popular ...

ADVE: Quite – but hardly outside restaurants, seaside resorts' and other spas' open-air concerts, and pre-talkie cinemas. No, Puccini's music agrees to be melodrama's handmaiden and nothing else. The ornamental and controlled virtuosities of *bel canto* are replaced by the unbridled outbursts, (*'espressivo* at all costs', as Nietzsche would have said), of *potente voce*. And it's mainly because potent singing voices, along with instrumental colours, are more easily and more palpably emotional and sensual than speech, that they are called in: to enlarge upon melodramatic effects – and preferably upon the simplest and crudest, such as sentimentality and violence.

ADVO: You're wildly, and – if I may say so – rather unfairly exaggerating. Any musician, even granting Puccini's scores no more than a perfunctory glance, cannot but find them full of musical qualities of no mean order. His scoring, for instance, is masterly. Never overladen, though powerful; and – a point that, given your leanings, should tell in his favour – much more often it follows the Franco-Russian style, Berlioz-cum-Rimsky-Korsakov, than the ponderous German tradition. And his manner of harmonizing, anything but academic, is decidedly on the modern side. Debussy's parallel 5ths and Dominant 9ths, Augmented 3rds derived from the whole-tone scale, and a bold linking of unrelated chords are no exceptions in Puccini's harmony, but constantly used, and with never-failing skill to vary and enrich his musical vocabulary and syntax.

Interlude I : A dialogue about Puccini

ADVE: I'm quite willing to grant that as a harmonist he is less naïvely platitudinous than as a melodist.

ADVO: You had better admire shrewd Puccini's making the best of both worlds: his melody sweeps the innocent listener off his feet; his harmony disarms the sophisticated theorist. And instead of sniffing at Puccini's sentimentality, ask yourself honestly whether the emotions released by the last act of *Bohème* are so very different from those released by more than one episode in Mahler's symphonies.

ADVE: They are indeed of the same brand – but that's a point down to Mahler, not a point up to Puccini. And – your turn to ask yourself a few questions about that making-the-best-of-both-worlds you are quite right to credit Puccini with – is it not (as in my opinion it is) a defect rather than a quality?

ADVO: I see I'll have to credit *you* with an extravagantly biased opinion – the sort the French call 'complaining about the bride's being too great a beauty'.

ADVE: Speaking of the French: after hearing *Tosca* in 1908 Paul Dukas with his usual unbiased good sense wrote that Puccini's music was 'well aimed and powerful', yet displayed 'harmonic oddities unwarranted by the music's more expressive context'. A very judicious remark. For with modern composers – a Debussy, a Webern, a Busoni – harmonic novelties, inventions, distortions and similar oddities were meant to be rebellious, ironic or allusive, and aimed, with an expostulation or a wink, at the inner circle of the attuned. Puccini, quite outside this inner circle, avails himself of these novelties and oddities, and uses them, out of context, as elements of musical luxury and chic. With the result that his pedestrian melody clad in Debussy's harmony resembles nothing so much as Leporello ill disguised under Don Giovanni's cloak. And the same remark applies to Puccini's exotic idioms, adumbrated in *Madam Butterfly,* and ridden to death in *Turandot.*

ADVO: Say what you will: it's not a defect but a quality in Puccini to have taken a few musical modernisms out of their esoteric limbo and into the open, and not to have been a confidential lyricist but a powerful dramatist.

ADVE: Well, I should have preferred to stick to my musician's last, but since you force me to appreciate our composer as a dramatist, I cannot but state that Puccini's dramatic *verismo* is exactly the same verity as Madame Tussaud's. Let's not linger with the unaccountable wax-figures that sing and move about the stage in *Madam Butterfly* – also musically the nadir of Puccini's production. *Tosca* is a horror play of the *Grand-Guignol* type: soft-hearted tigress killing and killed by pitch-black villain. Duration of the fight and the onlooker's delight: three acts. But even in a much better work, *Turandot* – much better not for its construction and general style but in detail, for its trios, its quintets and its often brilliant choral ensembles – what a sad and wicked bungling of Gozzi's classic comedy! Some years before Puccini started composing his last work, Busoni had treated the same subject in Gozzi's style, *viz*, with Mozartian economy and lightness. Puccini took the exactly opposite line: every scene is overworked; every episode needlessly repeated or protracted. A scene of torture and suicide is added – by then a standing feature in Puccini operas, but painfully out of place in a play that combines *commedia dell' arte* with *chinoiserie*, and calls for the spirit not of *verismo* and sentimentality but of fantasy and aloofness, and for some sort of puppet-show angularity of form and rhythm. But style is the last thing Puccini would care for. Let prima donna and tenor just be princess and prince, exactly true to life as Madame Tussaud would have them, and let them follow, at the top of their voices, the usual wavy flow of melodic triviality. In Gozzi, Turandot, defeated with her riddles, is allowed to win the second round. Her pride restored she can afford to surrender with ceremonious magnaminity. Puccini's Turandot remains thoroughly humiliated, and it's up to her victor's masterful *bacio* to do away, in no time, with her defloration complex, and bring about her surrender by very unceremonious methods. *Verismo* indeed – and perhaps an apt symbol of Puccini's ways with his public.

ADVO: There you are: to unceremonious Puccini the public surrenders night after night, *stagione* after *stagione*. Between 1898 and 1951, one thousand performances of *Bohème* at the Paris Opéra-Comique alone. And – I think I'll simply refer you to Goethe who says that none but remarkable qualities will secure popular favour for a long unbroken series of years. There are naïve opera goers, I'm told, who would never miss a performance of their adored *Bohème*, *Tosca* or *Butterfly*, and yet have never troubled to remember the composer's name. Isn't this anonymous fame the greatest imaginable?

Interlude I : A dialogue about Puccini

ADVE: I wonder. Hosts of naïve travellers adore staying in big cosmopolitan hotels which are just as luxurious and as comfortable to inhabit as Puccini operas, and have their lounges decorated, according to taste, with motives borrowed from Renoir, Matisse, Picasso or Henry Moore, or from Japanese prints – just as Puccini decorates his scores with harmonies borrowed from Debussy, or from others. Yet nobody has ever cared to know the names of the 'great architects' who have built those hotels. And, seriously, an element of democratic splendour and comfort is essential in Puccini. Classical Italian opera, and Verdi's and Berlioz's demand connoisseurs' awareness and attention. Of a Puccini opera's charm and appeal nothing is lost by listeners who simply undergo its alternately hypnotic and agitating effects. It would, by the way, be unjust not to add that in this respect, Puccini is Wagner's legitimate heir.

ADVO: You surprise me : everybody knows that, in Stendhal's day the connoisseurs came in, went out and talked a lot during a Cimarosa or Rossini performance.

ADVE: No doubt; but it was with them, by turns, total presence and total absence: for half an hour the *dilettanti* wouldn't listen at all, and then be rapturously attentive for five minutes. Puccini, on the contrary, allows and encourages (like Wagner) a continuous and pervading daydreamish half-listening. It is not by chance, I think, that his rise to fame immediately preceded the triumph of Hollywood. Emotional and sensual appeal, unassailable craftsmanship, psychological inanity and dubious taste: such are the marks of Puccini's as well as of Griffith's and Cecil B. de Mille's masterpieces. *La Fanciulla del West* is a Western among Westerns. But I wouldn't forget that the conclusion of this not-so-successful work of Puccini's contains perhaps his best music. All of a sudden it evokes that not merely emotional but moving atmosphere of negro spirituals – and, in 1909, who knew about negro spirituals?

ADVO: [*a little sardonically*] I suppose you are going to say that *Gianni Schicchi* is not so bad. And that Giacomo Puccini was a likable man.

ADVE: *Gianni Schicchi* is less cinematic and more purely operatic, than most of his operas, as well written as the best in *Turandot* and agreeably shorter. Yet as a successor to so many good comedies composed between Mozart's fifteenth and Verdi's eightieth birthday and as a contemporary of *L'Heure espagnole* and

Arlecchino, it does not occupy a very high rank. A likable man he certainly was, as a dedicated and perfect (and successful) craftsman rarely fails to be. And it is pleasant to think that most of his work (destined to stir up the nerves of town dwellers in quest of escapism) was done in a fishermen's village, betwixt sea and lake, day after day, until Giacomo interrupted his task to go for a walk with a beloved mistress, or – as far back as 1902 – for a drive in his beloved motor car.

ADVO: Stop trying to sweeten your acid comments. And since it falls to my lot to have the last word, I shall (quite superfluously) remark that, for another unbroken series of years, and whether the 'inner circle' like it or not, Puccini will be sung by famous singers, conducted by great conductors and welcomed as a glorious ...

ADVE: ... as a glorious potboiler by well advised managers ...

ADVO: ... as a glorious experience, vocal, orchestral and dramatic, by critics and experts, and by rank and file of opera-goers everywhere.

Puccini

7 Debussy in Italy: Respighi, Pizzetti, Malipiero, Casella

'Debussy, c'était Dieu!'
G. F. Malipiero

Some time ago Gian Francesco Malipiero, looking back on the beginning of his career at the turn of the century, declared: '... there was nothing doing in Milan, nothing in Bologna, etc, except a few indifferent experiments. I felt as though I was living in a musical desert.' An excellent Italian musicologist, Domenico de' Paoli, happened to be present – a descendant, by the way, of Boswell's famous Corsican friend. He smiled and said:

No, it was not *absolutely* a desert. There was, indeed, no 'movement', no 'school'. Several young musicians, however, were bent on getting away from melodrama and *verismo*, and had decided to write instrumental music, not after German models, as Sgambati, Rossi and Martucci had tried to do, but by contriving some sort of *nuova musica italiana*.

To explain the situation of Italian music in 1900, we have to remember the fact – inexplicable in itself – that no Italian symphonist, even of the comparatively modest stature of a Saint-Saëns or a D'Indy, appeared during the second half of the nineteenth century; only one great (and non-Italian) musician, Liszt, has to be thanked for introducing, in those days, all kinds of Italianisms into the vocabulary of his music. And even in the undisputedly Italian domain of opera there was by then only Verdi, an immensely popular, yet solitary giant.

71

F

But Verdi, who wrote the last romantic opera, *Otello*, and the last classical one, *Falstaff*, foreshadowed modernism also on two occasions: by composing a very unexpected opus, the *Pezzi Sacri*, and by making a very unexpected statement: 'Torniamo all' antico, e sarà un progresso.' Both *Pezzi* and 'Torniamo' were hardly meant to contain but in fact did contain *in nuce* all the convictions and techniques that were going to be hatched by Debussy's impending 'inconspicuous revolution': the 'static principle'; the archaizing reference to modal harmony and Gregorian melody; the craftsman's humility proclaimed, as opposed to romantic artist's pride; and classic *latinità* recommended, as oppose to Teutonic romanticism.

For an Italian musician, to be a musical patriot, a Latinist and an archaizer meant very much the same thing. Had not Palestrina and Pope Gregory been Italians? And had not, as Malipiero was pleased to recall in 1926, 'Claude Debussy studied, and loved, the other Claude, the one from Cremona' [viz Monteverde]?

Four composers were the first to embody the musical *Risorgimento*: Respighi, Pizzetti, Casella and Malipiero, and they were born and bound to be Debussyists. Yet – such is the force of *prima facie* characteristics – it was at first, not so much by D'Annunzio's friend, the essential, latinizing and Monteverdean Debussy, that they were going to let themselves be encouraged and influenced, but by Debussy the impressionist. Respighi owes his place in the symphonic repertoire to two arch-impressionist scores, *Fontane di Roma* (1917), and *Pini di Roma* (1925), the latter one famous for adding a grain of surrealist salt to impressionism: the recording of a nightingale's actual twitterings being provided for every performance by Messrs Ricordi and Company, along with the other orchestral parts. Pizzetti's *La Pisanella* (1911) is another piece of impenitent impressionism, and so is his *Concerto dell' Estate* (1928), written in the composer's forty-ninth year. *Impressioni dal Vero* – birdsong again, but unrecorded – is one of Malipiero's early symphonic works (1911). Casella, it is true, had had his pre-Debussyist day – not without misgivings, veiled by irony: 'I offer two solid symphonies for sale [he wrote in a programme note]: they are written in the German, Straussian and Mahlerian tradition. Unoriginality guaranteed – and that's why I want to sell them.' One of these scores was – nationalism nascent – the rhapsody *Italia*, which quotes *Funiculì, funicula*, and (owing to subject matter

rather than composer's temperament) indeed resembles Strauss'
Aus Italien. But presently the spell worked: he wrote *L'Adieu à la
Vie* (for voice and piano, 1915), *Pagine de Guerra* (same date), and
A Notte Alta (1917) for piano, and his personality was set free – by
Debussy.

Respighi and Pizzetti

Among the four pioneers there is a certain affinity in type and
character between Respighi and Pizzetti. With them craftsmanship
stands out. Their technique is as impeccable as Puccini's, their taste
incomparably better, and their popular appeal proportionately
feebler. Born (1879) in Bologna, Ottorino Respighi came from a
family whose members' avocations and activities had been of
uncommon diversity. His father was a civil servant, his grandfather
a violinist, and Verdi's friend. Other Respighis were dignitaries of
the Vatican. Young Ottorino, aged nine, began his musical studies
as a violinist, and showed considerable gift: at twenty he won his
diploma with Paganini's redoubtable *Streghe*. Meanwhile he had
started composing, and so successfully that his teacher, Martucci,
congratulated by a friend for his pupil's accomplishments,
smilingly retorted: 'My dear, Respighi is not a pupil: è un
maestro.' The maestro in question accepted an appointment as
leader of an orchestra in St Petersburg, and had the excellent idea
of resuming lessons in composition for five weeks with Rimsky-
Korsakov. Two years later in Berlin it was perhaps Ottorino the
violinist who made Ottorino the composer attend the composition
class of Max Bruch, writer of post-romantic violin concertos of
dubious quality and undeservedly remembered even today. Small
wonder if Respighi admitted later on that his last teacher had not
influenced him at all. On the other hand, Debussy's influence, so
manifest in Respighi's subsequent symphonic works, remained unacknowledged, though it can hardly have been unconscious.

The same applies to Ildebrando Pizzetti, born in Parma (1880), of
whom his friend Guido M. Gatti, the founder and editor of *La
Rassegna Musicale*, wrote in 1926 that 'perhaps alone among the
Italian composers of his time, Pizzetti was deaf to the impressionist
sirens' song' – a statement flatly contradicted by a good number of
Pizzetti's scores. His style – again according to Gatti – 'is opposed
to modern disillusionment and irony, and rooted in the idealism of

73

his religious and moral convictions'. Unfortunately, as André Gide was wont to remark, superior ways of feeling do not necessarily foster superior works of art. Pizzetti became a practical, practised and most distinguished member of his profession, one of Nature's academicians, and better known abroad as the chairman of the Accademia di Santa Cecilia (1948-51) than as a champion of spiritual values.

Both Respighi and Pizzetti were keen revivers and transcribers of Italian music of the past. Pizzetti edited madrigals by Gesualdo and sonatas by Veracini. Respighi won Nikisch's favour with a transcription of Monteverde's *Lamento d'Arianna*: *Torniamo all' Antico* indeed.

They are both very unequal composers, and their inequalities are always of style, never of technique. Pizzetti's Cello Sonata, although certainly a remarkable work, advances curiously from its rhetorical espressivo opening towards a much better, dissonant and agitated middle section and a slow finale, interesting for its bell-like sound and *Cathédrale-engloutie* atmosphere. And in Respighi's and Pizzetti's astonishingly similar, lively and even feverishly *concitato* manner of writing opera, composer's sincerity and dramatist's gentlemanly sense of not overdoing effects do not quite make up for this style's oscillations between romantic *cliché*, Wagnerian chromaticism and modern-archaic modal evocation. Such are – with their meritoriously unrealistic librettos – Pizzetti's *Fedra* (after D'Annunzio, not Racine) and Respighi's *La Fiamma*, full of witchcraft and cruelty. Pizzetti, however, who outlived Respighi (died 1936) by more than a generation's time space, achieved with *Murder in the Cathedral* (1958), written in his seventy-ninth year, a style of much greater unity and purity without loss of dramatic strength.

At some other moment of the history of music, when it was safe for any composer to embark upon his voyage because the vessels of form and style were ready at hand and seaworthy, and the compass in his pocket the same as every other composer's, nothing would have prevented Respighi and Pizzetti from being composers of the rank of Pergolesi or Corelli, if not a Vivaldi. But in our century when composers have, in Herbert Read's words, 'to build every one his personal raft to cross the stream', they were at cross-purposes with the situation. Conventionalists by temperament they had, by position in time, to be innovators. There was no convention to feed their conventionalism, and their innovations were destined to fall short of novelty.

Malipiero

Gian Francesco Malipiero's music, on the contrary, is unconventional to the point of being hard to classify or even to describe. The strangeness – a source of delight or irritation, according to the listener's habits, temperament and disposition – is certainly compelling: so much so that in 1913, at the composers' competition in Rome it conquered an unwilling and unwitting jury. As often happens on such occasions most of the adjudicators were the sort who disapprove of the strange and the unconventional. They knew about Malipiero – then aged thirty-one – and his contribution was turned down without ceremony. But he had submitted four other scores under fictitious names, and the four Malipieros-in-disguise were awarded the four available prizes. 'Ce fut un épouvantable scandale' said De' Paoli when he told me about this adventure.

Always a composer, but at times also a farmer and gardener, Malipiero was the offspring of an old Venetian family, with a musician or two and also a doge or two among his ancestors. He lived in Asolo, a very pleasant townlet not very far from Venice and not very far up the Treviso mountains. After having first studied in Venice and in Bologna, he went to Vienna – to escape 'the desert' – then to Berlin, where he met Busoni, and finally to Paris, where he met Casella, D'Annunzio, Ravel and Stravinsky – and became for ever a disciple of Debussy's – the most enthusiastically faithful, and perhaps with Stravinsky, the most independent of Debussyists. Soon he turned away from impressionist Debussy, to the archaizing and adventurously bold and modern composer of the *Études* and *Sonates* – the Debussy who was influenced, as Malipiero quite justifiably thought, by Monteverde, 'that other Claude' who, next to Debussy, was going to be the prime figure in Malipiero's musical household.

Debussyist Gian Francesco, moreover, never had to liberate himself from Debussy. From the first his independence was inscribed in his character and in his manner of being a composer. It was Debussy's fate always to remain, for all his anti-romanticism, a tragic solitary deliverer of sparse long-meditated *ultima verba*. Malipiero – head for more than a decade of the famous Accademia

Benedetto Marcello in Venice, and yet without noteworthy disciples – was also no doubt an isolated musician – but not a solitary one. He may have been without companions; his style is nothing if not companionable.

His numerous works sound as though they were produced like *quattrocento* paintings in Malipiero's (imaginary) atelier with imaginary assistants working under the maestro's supervision. Such is their relaxed manner that nothing is obtrusively personal about their expression. Their originality of technique and style is equally unobtrusive, and often looks like the originality of a school rather than of an individual artist.

Companionable Malipiero chose to compose a series of *Dialoghi*. Dialogues in more than one sense: between instruments and between polyphonic lines to begin with; but also dialogues between their composer and other composers – or their ghosts. As an editor of Monteverde's collected works Malipiero knew everything about this sort of conversation with the past, about its fascination and about its melancholy. So, casting his spell, he summoned Jacopone da Todi (that heretical composer of thirteenth century *Laude*, imprisoned by one pope, released by another one), and 'Magister Josephus' i.e. Zarlino (1507–90), a Venetian theorist of the diatonic scale and, therefore, a born patron of the anti-chromatic branch of musical modernists. And these *Dialoghi*, vocal and instrumental, are full of Monteverde-isms, and full of Malipierian strangeness – and, moreover, strangely moving.

Though Malipiero has his workshop and school complete with tools, rules and secrets, there was never anything systematic about his methods. His symphonies, for example – seven in number (1933–48) but, characteristically preceded (long before: 1905–10) and followed (shortly afterwards: 1950–1) by two pairs of others – are probably some of the very few twentieth-century symphonies that are devoid of Beethovenisms – devoid of protracted developments as well as of *sinfonica-eroica* accents. They are mostly symphonic fantasies in four short movements. Not a few allusions to *concerto-grosso* style are met with: in the *Quinta Sinfonia* two pianos start proceedings with a canon reminiscent of the last *Brandenburg* Concerto. The themes of the Third Symphony (*delle campani*: of bells) extol the 'static principle'. Malipiero's own description of the Seventh runs as follows: '. . . bears the sub title: "of songs", because this symphony is absolutely linear. Here and

there a kind of song emerges : it might be the voice of some antique
poet singing from the heights of the sacred Mount Grappa, while
beyond, far away, always further away, lies Venice.' As to syntax
and structure we find lightness and transparency everywhere, and
often a Stravinskian toying with favoured intervals. Polytonality
occurs at times. From the First Symphony to the Seventh the
frequency of non-blending dissonance increases. Loose symmetries
of form and seeming improvisation do not impair unity of construction, thanks to the 'touch of the school' – in other words, thanks to
Malipiero's uncanny vividness of imagination, which infuses life
even into near-formalistic formulas.

Malipiero would not have been Malipiero without an endearing
and impish streak of eccentricity – an Italian variant of Charles
Kœchlin's. His music, his sayings and writings, his smile and, at
times, his guffaw betrayed his awareness of the paradox and
comedy of his situation as an aristocratic, isolated craftsman and a
soliloquizing dialogist. And, indeed, no disciple of Debussy's can be
caught writing – eighteenth century fashion – symphonies by the
half-dozen, and keep a straight face: 'The First Symphony . . .
dates from 1933. Originally it was named First and Last Symphony.
But this title was too great a pledge. . . .' Only a jester at Cleo-
patra's court – *vide* Shakespeare, and Constant Lambert: 'Music
Ho!' – would carry a composer's mock-innocence and mock-
disillusionment to the point of calling an (excellent) piece of music
Silence Interrupted (*Pausa del Silenzio*, 1917) – the most anti-
idealistic definition of music's *raison d'être* ever put forward? And
none but Malipiero would have dreamed of qualifying an *elegia* as
a *capriccio* (1951). Or of writing – long before Benjamin Britten's
Young Person's Guide was issued – a symphonic score (*Concerti*,
1931), whose movements are so many double-concertos for strings,
and then wood-wind, and then percussion, and then brass –
beginning with a fantasy on tuning-up, and leading up to a diminutive concerto (sixty bars) for big bad double-basses. By the way :
this theme of tuning-up, treated off-handedly and with Italian
gusto (as opposed to the respectful ceremoniousness of a similar
evocation in Alban Berg's Violin Concerto) recurs in Malipiero's
Rispetti e Strambotti, no doubt the wittiest string quartet written in
our day and an exemplary one for its never-flagging vivaciousness
of motive, rhythm and counterpoint.

Malipiero's operatic style, blending *Pelléas* and *La Boîte à*

joujoux with *L'Incoronazione di Poppea* and *Il Ballo delle Ingrate,*
is – small wonder – better equipped to enchant an audience of
sophisticated musicians than an opera house full of naïve opera-
goers. Yet lovers of both opera and Venice cannot but be carried
away by the *Commedie Goldoniane* (written in 1925, with other
Venetian entertainments to follow). If Venetian interplay of mask
and *morbidezza* has ever connived at being echoed in music,
Malipiero has brilliantly succeeded. And later (1934) *La Favola del
Figlio Cambiato*, on Pirandello's text, is Venetian at one remove:
masks masking masks, and *morbidezza* organized and defying
psychoanalysis.

Venetianism, indeed, is Malipiero's ultimate test and *virtù*. And
Malipiero's manner will not cease to mean a lot to those who enjoy
an art that knows how to fit idioms of perfect artificiality into a
discourse of perfect naturalness.

Casella

If, side by side with Venetian Malipiero, Piedmontese Casella had
not existed, the History of Music or the *genius loci* would have had
to invent him as a perfect complementary figure. After any first
performance of his latest score Malipiero would ask: 'Do you
really like that piece of mine?' Casella was no more presumptuous
than Malipiero. Yet on similar occasions he would unfailingly tell
us: 'I'm sure that's one of my best'. Malipiero, a composer and
nothing else, is aristocratic, countrified, self-contained, Shakespearian, – elvish and 'fantastical', never predictable. Casella –
composer, conductor, and concert pianist, a chamber-music player
and a teacher – was a town dweller and a musician of the world,
professional horse-sense all over, rational, extrovert and practical.

Born in Turin (1883) Alfredo Casella belonged to a family of
musicians: three well known cellists in two generations, his mother
a pianist. Believers in hereditary talent and virtue have (not quite
successfully) tried to trace his lineage back to Pietro Casella, a
composer of madrigals (all of them lost), and Dante's friend. However, Alfredo Casella's musical upbringing was mainly French. A
brilliant pupil at the Paris Conservatoire – with Fauré for composition – he was for some time deputy professor of Cortot's piano
class. As a young conductor he championed Mahler – a lost cause:
in 1910 scores of inordinate length had no chance with French

listeners, who – with a better grasp of native punning than of foreign spelling – would soon nickname long, lanky and beaky Alfredo *l'oiseau de malhe(u)r*.

It was not by chance, if Casella had noticed – and in those days he was almost the only one capable of noticing – that in spite of unbridgeable dissimilitude of style and musical outlook Debussy and Mahler had something in common : a preference for simplified and un-romantically diatonic melody and a taste for clothing or framing such melody in unusual instrumental colours. Casella was apt to bring together musical styles far apart in space or time. He stands thereby nearer to Ravel and to Dukas, and to Stravinsky, than to any other follower of Debussy. But in contrast to Dukas or Ravel his familiarity with a thousand scores neither discouraged Casella the composer nor reduced his production. He was never in quest of adventurous novelty in music. For him a modern musician's task was not to sow but to reap. He edited Bach's preludes and fugues, Beethoven's piano sonatas and Clementi's symphonies; scored Bach's Chaconne in D minor, Balakirev's *Islamey* and marches by Schubert, and fitted themes of Scarlatti's and Paganini's into a piano concerto and an orchestral fantasy. Travelling with his trio from Rome to London, and from London to Paris, Dresden, Leipzig and Vienna, he ransacked the music library of every town for forgotten Vivaldi or Geminiani manuscripts. He wrote a pamphlet on Stravinsky, an exhaustive book on the evolution of keyboard playing over two centuries and a most original one on the evolution of the tonal cadence in Western music. And his composing was perfectly consistent with his activities as an instrumentalist, a traveller, and a writer.

Casella, most spontaneously, combined scepticism with gusto. modern rootlessness with French classicism, be it ever so battered. And he had the Italians' unwillingness to wallow, like those metaphysical (i.e. mad) Northerners, in the tragic insolubility of tragic problems. Bach and Rameau are at hand, and Liszt, and the Russians, and the old Italians and the modern French, and so are Ravel's and Dukas's methods for dealing with them all : Casella's music is derivative in its vocabulary, yet unmistakably personal in its robust elegance, full of musician's *joie de vivre*, and always crediting its listeners with intelligence, and often with a sense of fun.

Such is his early chamber music – *Siciliana e Burlesca* (flute and piano, or piano trio) and *Pupazzetti* (piano duet) – the very first music, in fact, of the sort so eagerly welcomed, about 1925, by Satie followers and other young composers after the First World War – Křenek, Kurt Weil, Lord Berners, Walton (*Façade*), Poulenc: music that defies the traditionalist's upturned nose without showing more respect for the rebel's puckered brow. Or *in modo serio* there are his most rewarding piano pieces, the *Sei Studi*, Op. 70 (1944), *Ricercari* on *BACH*, Op. 52 – uncommonly witty inventions on this much-laboured theme – and *Sinfonia, Arioso e Toccata* (Op. 59) with a convincing example of 'synthetic melody' in the manner of the Adagio of Ravel's G major Concerto in its middle section. Often, as in his Cello Sonata No. 2 (Op. 45) and in his Concerto for piano, strings and percussion (Op. 69), Casella, giving neo-classicism, *ostinato* semiquavers and *motorik* their due, would sound, if you can imagine that sort of style, like unpedantic Hindemith or non-barbaric Prokofiev.

His ballet music (*La Giara*, 1924) is both Debussyist and Ravelian again. So is, alongside his (necessarily) archaizing *Favola di Orfeo* (1932), his fantastic opera *La Donna Serpente* (same date), a masterpiece of vocal virtuosity, of transparent polyphony, of bright orchestral colours: exquisitely proportioned, and delightful from beginning to end, but of course dismissed as 'concert-goers' music' by all the wise men of operatic Gotham.

But it is difficult to discover the reason why similarly wise men fail to recommend Casella's *Missa solemnis pro pace* (1944) – certainly, as he would have said, 'one of the best' scores his enthusiasm and his mastery ever achieved.

Alfredo Casella died in 1947 – untiring till the last, in spite of cruel ill health, as a *Defensor Musices*, a defender of every composer, ancient or modern, worth defending, from Monteverde to Dallapiccola.

'You have known him, as I have,' said Malipiero, 'as a great musician and a lovable companion. But, believe me, he was not so very far from being a saint. In a musical world of competition and envy he was disinterestedness, kindness and intelligent sympathy personified.'

Interlude 11:
Picturesque and essential Busoni

Next to Debussy's, the most telling influence on the new Italian
school – on Casella, on Malipiero, on young Dallapiccola – was no
doubt Busoni's: an influence that would have turned out to be
even greater, and easier to trace, if Busoni had not been so mobile a
figure, if many had not found it difficult to make their choice
among the fleeting and contradictory aspects of his strange genius.

His fame as a pianist has long stood in the way of his recognition
as a composer. The romantically minded often disagreed with his
unsentimental way of looking at Bach or Beethoven for architecture of rhythm and sound rather than for eloquence and emotion,
but all who ever heard him agreed that there was something
fantastic, magical, almost diabolic about his playing. Two testi-
monials – the first to his powers, the second to his imagination – are
worth rescuing from oblivion. On the night following an uncommonly hot midsummer day he appeared at a symphony concert
given in the vast crowded casino of a seaside resort. After the
concerto the applause would not ebb until Busoni, rather grumpily,
sat down again for an encore. Suddenly a flash of malice passed
over his face: the programme had started with the *Tannhäuser*
Overture; Busoni with the glee of a conjuring Mephistopheles
attacked that same overture in Liszt's transcription – and a witness
of that concert told me long afterwards that the luminosity, the
ever-varied colours of his playing, the breathtaking vivacity of his
phrasing, made the resources of trombones, clarinets and all
Wagner's fiddles in the orchestra's previous performance recede
into drabness and dullness.

About twenty years later Busoni began to dislike playing more and more. He liked his composition class which gathered in his home for long discussions between pupils and between master and pupils. One night he wound up: 'I know you quite enjoy all this talk, yet I suspect you would prefer it if, for a change, I played for you.' 'Oh . . . yes, maestro!' And Busoni started playing scales, went on playing scales, played nothing but scales for a very long time. 'And', added Arthur Lourié, the Russian composer then Busoni's pupil, 'it was perhaps the greatest piano playing I ever came across. He played scales of every description and beyond description – tranquil scales and agitato scales, light scales and compact scales, adagios and scherzos of scales, scales that fell like rain, and scales that rose like flames. It was like watching a Renoir prepare his palette.'

Ferruccio Benvenuto was the son of Ferdinando Busoni, a well-known but undisciplined clarinet player (who, 'bearded, whiskered and wellingtoned, looked like a stableman or a lion-tamer', and never agreed to sit in an orchestra and follow a conductor's beat) and a well-known and disciplined pianist ('in the Thalberg tradition: very fluent and a bit drawing-roomish') who in the spring of 1866 played in Liszt's presence in Rome, a week before Ferruccio's birth in Empoli.

In this small Tuscan town, very much like the one depicted in *Where Angels fear to tread*, a famous popular ceremony used to take place on Corpus Christi. On stout ropes a live jackass, provided with a shapely pair of golden wings, was lowered from the roof of the campanile – a festive mockery addressed to the burghers of neighbouring Volterra, who had declared that donkeys would fly before Empoli would beat them. After which, of course, the Empolitans had to be victorious without delay, and Busoni, later on, to be impatient of wingless asses.

Towards 1870 Madame Busoni and her son settled down in her father's house in Trieste. Quite sensibly her husband had decided to spare her, for a while, the troubles of his bohemian style of life. Grandfather Giuseppe Weiss, a mariner of German origin, had eventually settled down in Trieste, married an Italian and become a respected citizen. He disapproved of his son-in-law, who called him an *assassino* in return, and one evening in 1872 Ferdinando appeared in Trieste to recover – and, as he believed, rescue – wife and child. Such was the unquiet scene of Ferruccio's beginnings.

Regularly schooled by his mother and erratically by his father, he gave his first concert at the age of seven. He played his first piano compositions aged ten, and aged twelve conducted a *Stabat mater* written in W.A. Remy's then renowned composition class. But there was nothing challenging, let alone rebellious, about his near-Mozartian precocity: a string quartet, written a little later, shows amazing command of form and material; its style is exactly Mendelssohn's and early Schumann's. He soon won international renown by playing the whole conventional repertoire, and taught at the Conservatoires of Helsingfors, Moscow and Boston.

Then his approach to music began to change. He still performed a lot of Liszt, and discovered and perfected his singular manner of treating the piano. With him the opening deep G's of Liszt's Sonata sounded, we are told, like the pizzicati of half a dozen double basses. He lost part of his interest in Chopin: 'a great composer but one who owes his prestige with the public to a sentimentality he shared with much lesser ones'. He played (and edited and transcribed) more and more Bach, and revived Mozart's then half-forgotten concertos. He was among the first to protest against the generally accepted view that among the classics 'elegant and divine', Mozart's main importance was to be 'great and human' Beethoven's forerunner. For Busoni 'had learned a most difficult thing: to distinguish between good and bad Beethoven', and to admit 'that a Sonata, Op. 106, and a C sharp minor Quartet certainly outweigh his symphonies'. He had 'let himself be overwhelmed by Berlioz'; 'had hated, then admired, and in the end, – as befits a Latin – turned away from, Wagner'; 'discovered the new French, then dropped them when they became popular too fast'; and 'finally got much nearer to the old Italian dramatists.'

In 1901, Busoni completed his Second Sonata for violin and piano, Op. 36a, 'but to be considered as my Op. 1' – a work still in the romantic (especially the Franckist) line, but displaying for the first time a typical Busoni fingerprint: unorthodox cadences that result from wayward interlinking of chords that are in themselves quite innocent. His Piano Concerto (Op. 39, 1903–4) followed, a tasteful, and tasty, and a very unusual work, but not yet a very original one, except for the fact that it never condescends to meretricious effects in spite of demanding super-Lisztian virtuosity, and that for all the monumentality of its proportions it almost sounds like chamber music.

And then, in 1910, comes a score that seems to have been written by another composer: the *Berceuse élégiaque*, Op. 42 – 'a piece in which for the first time I contrived to find my own sound, and make form and musical feeling coincide'; and a piece that, static and 'atmospheric' as it is, fully deserved its French name, though Busoni emphasized that in his *Élégie* perhaps similar results were obtained by methods quite different from Debussy's. 'Debussy,' he said, 'is a harmonist who has found his way. I am a polyphonist in quest of his way.'

In quest of his way, indeed, and mapping it out, for meanwhile (in the manner of old Rameau) Busoni, before embarking upon his main works, had framed the theory that was going to warrant and inform his new musical practice. He published (1907) his *Entwurf eine neuen Aesthetik der Tonkunst* – a title hard to translate. Let's say: *Aesthetics of music reconsidered: a draft.* Never was a shorter treatise on music written nor a less scholastic one. In fact a manifesto against every sort of musical scholasticism and routine, against all the uncritically accepted musical conventions and taboos. 'Music is a miraculous child. Uncalled-for legislators have fettered it. Take the chains away!' (Quite unknown to, and unacquainted with, Busoni in 1907, Monsieur Croche whole-heartedly agreed.) 'Why have composers, for centuries, been content with only two scales, major and minor? Why have they accepted stereotyped cadences and other permanent devices of construction like sonata form? How much better when Beethoven takes to free improvisation, as in the pages preceding the fugue of Op. 106!' And, like all nonconformists that are no prigs aware of the wisdom of paradox, Busoni suggests that the purest moments of music are to be found in pauses and fermatas and in the tension 'well known to great performers' that inhabits the silence between the end of one movement and the beginning of the next. 'Why, again, have composers agreed to sort consonant sheep from dissonant goat? And agreed to be influenced by the *clichés* of instrumental mannerisms – by the cello's excessive vibrato, the oboe's hesitant attack, the clarinet's boastful eloquence, the trombone's spurious depth?' And so narrow is the range of musical invention between tonic and dominant that 'one afternoon it took no time to discover about fifteen themes, some taken from good scores, some from very bad ones, but all fit to be played together with the second theme of the Adagio of the Ninth Symphony'.

After having denounced all such time-honoured addiction to

musical laziness, Busoni tells us how to escape from the treadmill, and anticipates almost every device, every experiment resorted to and attempted between his day and ours :

Polymodalism : 113 modes may be obtained by every imaginable distribution of sharps, flats and naturals on the seven degees of the diatonic scale;

Polytonality : for example, any of these fancy modes combined with traditional C major, A minor, E flat major, etc;

Micro-intervals : sixth-tones obtained from two sets of third-tones, one between C and its octave, the other one between C sharp and its octave. Busoni had an harmonium tuned in this manner, and liked to puzzle some listeners posted in the next room, who never failed to mistake the eighteen-note chromatic octave for the usual twelve-note one – proof, said Busoni, of the third-tone's validity and 'naturalness';

New orchestral ensembles, with greater scope given to bells, gongs and other percussion;

New instruments, or rather new timbres electro-mechanically produced : Busoni describes and recommends a vast machine, the *Dynamophone* 'that looks like an engine room', has been devised to combine at every possible pitch, fundamentals and harmonics in every proportion chosen, and has been actually constructed, 'at excessive costs, unfortunately', in America, by Dr Thaddeus Cahill. No doubt, *concrete* and electronic music pre-visited.

Multi-faceted Busoni, unafraid of being disconcerting and on occasion self-contradictory, did not resort to micro-intervals or to Dr Cahill's engine room in any of his compositions. Even without them his style was anti-conformist enough. He would never cast two scores in the same mould – Ravel's or Stravinsky's attitude already, and a most exceptional attitude at a time when Strauss, Reger or Mahler, no more than Sibelius or Elgar, ever had any qualms about repeating themselves. And, owing to his experimental scales and to their frequently fanciful lay-out, all his scores have a Berliozian air of unruly baroque boldness. Moreover Busoni – wont to perform, revive and transcribe Bach, Mozart, Liszt and Beethoven – was no less given to showing his gratitude towards the past of music than to abhorring the chains imposed by tradition. And with typical clarity of insight he vindicated this dividedness of tendency and called it *Junge Klassizität* (not to be translated as neo-classicism)'.

'Classical Approach Rejuvenated', said Busoni, 'means the ability to master, to sift and to avail oneself of all the experience, all the experiments, past or present ... The art we are after shall be both old and novel. And (fortunately, I think) the destiny of music today carries us all in that direction, whether we are conscious of it or not, and whether we like it or not.' Busoni distrusted, 'as befits a Latin' (he could again have said) the Romantics' conspicuous, unqualified musical revolution. He was interested in Schoenberg; he edited one of Schoenberg's piano pieces in order to make its then very shocking atonal harmonies easier for unprepared listeners to grasp; and as early as in pre-dodecaphonic 1916 he wrote a fully fledged and most apparent twelve-tone row : the opening fanfare of *Arlecchino*. But he found in Schoenberg's music '... an almost barbarous amount of naïvety – and again plenty of things that are free and easy, and prove his perspicacity and sincerity. ...' – a most unexpected view in 1911 when the reproach of over-sophistication and, of course, of 'intellectualism' was incessantly hurled at Schoenberg as well as at Busoni himself. Indeed, to hear another perspicacious composer tax Schoenberg with anything approaching naïvety, we shall have to wait for Boulez.

Written between 1910 and 1921 the six Sonatinas, the Toccata for piano and *Romanza e scherzoso*, Op. 54, for piano and orchestra are singularly successful attempts at that classico-modern synthesis Busoni was after. Most imaginative, impressionist-and-beyond keyboard writing blended with homages to Italianate, Lisztian melody and with severe, even pitiless polyphony invented by the most intelligent and the most delightfully perverse disciple of Bach's 'Free and easy' dissonance and unexpected and unprepared consonance – and not a grain of naïvety. Music aimed – like humour, wit and irony in Mr Fowler's classification – at 'the sympathetic', 'the intelligent' and 'an inner circle', and therefore respectfully held at arm's length by Rachmaninov-minded (or Poulenc-minded) performers.

During the same decade Busoni's ideas about the opera – also laid down in the *Entwurf* – gave birth to three masterpieces: *Turandot*, *Arlecchino*, and *Doktor Faust*.

'Dramatic characters that sing: the most anti-realistic of conventions. Therefore, to justify and compensate one impossibility by another one, operatic plays should consist of unlikely, varied and incredible situations, conflicts and events.' That precludes any sort of realism on the operatic stage, let alone *verismo*.

'Love scenes are out of place in opera. No more than, in real life, lovers' conversation should be witnessed by any *terzo incommodo*, the public should be given the *terzo incommodo*'s part in the opera house.'

That disposes of nine operas out of ten – and, incidentally, explains why opera managers are not so eager to admit Busoni's to the repertoire.

Where, in operas, should music come in? Music should never try to depict, to duplicate, things that are anyhow perceptible in the theatre. Music should come in with marches and pageants, with dances, with ballads and other songs that fall into the characters' roles, and whenever the supernatural enters the scene. For the unnatural and the supernatural are the two elements of an imaginary world which opera has to reflect in its comic mirror and in its magic mirror.

In consequence *Turandot* (after Gozzi) borrows its style from *The Arabian Nights*, the puppet show and the *commedia dell' arte*. The action is reduced to essentials. Exoticism is adumbrated with utter discretion, and so is the spirit of irony and the spirit of farce. Vocal writing owes a lot to Mozart, little to *bel canto* and nothing at all to *potente voce* (see page 66). Diatonic melody is sustained by fancy-modal winking and squinting harmonization, of which the use of the F sharp major triad as a dominant in C major is an instance, and as it were the symbol. *Chinoiseries* are mostly bad enough, and musical *chinoiseries* worse. *Turandot* is excellent.

Arlecchino, also derived from the *commedia dell' arte*, is more complex: a *morality*, a musical entertainment and an operatic parody. The protagonist, a speaking role and an autobiographical one – Busoni made no bones about his being half Arlecchino, half Faust – is a lean, impish, aristocratic moralist and immoralist who, just to show his virtuosity, takes his townsfolk – the gullible, the complacent, the xenophobe, and the inane – to task while exposing with loving contempt the impossible opera's delightful impossibilities.

On morals Arlecchino to Columbina, 'Faithfulness, Madam, means betrayal of the countless other opportunities,' (If Busoni banned the love-duet, it was not for puritanical reasons.)

Regarding tradition and virtue: the tailor (Arlecchino's pet cuckold) quotes Dante: *Galeazzo fu il libro* (*Don Giovanni* quoted in the orchestra) 'Ah ... yes! Unchastity, thou art the real Pandar'.

On the legitimate opera Colombina to Leandro, who clothes his courting in coloratura triplets: 'Do you think that's good taste?' (Follows a parody of the last *Fidelio* finale.)

As to the music itself, *Arlecchino* is probably the best polyphony written for the stage between *Falstaff* and Britten at his most proficient.

Busoni, like every other musician, loved Mozart's *Magic Flute*, and, like Goethe and a few others, admired Schikaneder's *Zauber-flöte* libretto, which was indeed as Busoni wanted them to be: made up of the 'unnatural' or the only-too-natural (Papageno, Monostatos) and the 'supernatural' – or the spiritual (Sarastro), and apt to be reflected in the opera's comic and magic mirrors.

Doktor Faust, musically most unlike *Die Zauberflöte*, is nevertheless operatically similar. A huge mystery play, mainly about Faust-the-Magician – only the last act is Faust-the-Sage's – and dramatic throughout. Not a drama, like Wagner's, devised to be accompanied underlined and exalted by music, but a drama to be embodied by music, and meant to have its beginning, its end, its *raison d'être* in the score. For example it all starts with Faust's being provided with The Book that is going to make him a magician. Just as in *Die Zauberflöte* three charming ladies turn up with Tamino's flute and Papageno's chime, three very polite students from Cracow will bring the book as a present for Dr Faust, Rector Magnificus of the University of Wittenberg. That's the action 'visible, anyhow, in the theatre' and it's up to the music to show how disquieting these students are – Hell's emissaries in fact. In the next scene Faust, book in hand and magic circle drawn, calls up the Spirits, to choose the one that will serve him. And again it's the test of music that provides the test of magic: Faust asks for the speediest of spirits, and the whole scene shall be a progression of tempo, from the first spirit 'slow as the sand in the hourglass', up to the sixth, Mephistopheles, whose prestissimo 'equals the speed of man's thought'.

Faust surrenders. But his signing of the pact with the powers of Darkness is only one half of that moment's polyphony – the other half being the many-voiced *Credo*, sung during the Easter Sunday Service, off stage: an extraordinary shaping of tragic point into musical contrast. And, later on, Faust's dealings with his German students culminate, once more, in counterpoint: the Protestants intone Luther's hymn; at once the Catholics counter, first, with a

Te Deum, and then – let's prove anti-puritans! – with a ribald madrigal.

The magician's recital at the Duke of Parma's court – a second play within the main play – is another virtuoso piece of operatic polyphony. And the two scenes that come nearest to being love-scenes are also scenes of magic: when the Duchess, a spell-bound sleep-walker, responds to Faust's incantation; and, in the next act, when the elusive Helen of Troy is summoned up. And, to quote one more episode of Busoni's baroque play, the magic of the mounte-bank sort commands the Berliozian *ballata*: Mephistopheles dashes in, and throws a dead baby – Faust's and the Duchess' child – at Faust's feet. He then convinces the indignant and terri-fied onlookers that there is no baby at all, live or dead: nothing but a rag doll – 'rather a clumsy counterfeit'.

In the last act magic leads to metaphysics – a domain hard to translate into those palpable images of unreality Busoni so saga-ciously wanted opera to consist of. Faust, about to die, accepts that mortal fallible Faust should have been a mere passing torchbearer of 'Faust, an eternal will'. A magician to the last, he reverses Mephistopheles's mendacious illusionism and revives his child. A little less felicitously, he also revives *art nouveau* symbolism by making his chosen successor 'a naked adolescent, walk townwards through the snowlit night, a flowering branch in his hand'.

But then – unless composed by Mozart, opera has never failed to be imperfect. *Doktor Faust* is no less essential a moment in twentieth-century music for not being more perfect than *Pelléas*. By 1920 Busoni's music was the first avantgarde music that did not stem from Debussy or (by way of the Viennese) from Wagner. Though it refers to so dazzling (and puzzling) a variety of sources, it stems mainly – in manner rather than matter – from Berlioz and late Beethoven (sometimes by way of Italianate Liszt). It has opened a third, baroque, strange and independent style of being a modern musician. With the result that musicians as dissimilar as Philip Jarnach, Varèse, and Kurt Weill, Boris Blacher, Vladimir Vogel and Nicolas Nabokov, Stravinsky and Britten, Arthur Lourié and Ronald Stevenson, would – all of them for a lifetime, a decade, a year or a day – follow Busoni, or one of his aspects, or several.

'A polyphonist in quest of his way' – and a polyphonic persona-lity. Also, until 1924, the year of his death, an ever searching and ever adventurous writer of essays and fascinating letters, like those he addressed on tour to his charming Swedish wife whom, *pace* Arlecchino, he adored: portraying people he had met, appraising London and Paris before the war and after, or expatiating, in typical paradox or unforeseen commonsense on the latest French or English book he was reading. Or telling her about his latest, presumably Italian or German, dream:

Last night I saw beings of an unknown race – whether animal or human I would not decide. They were small, about the size of squirrels. Their bodies looked like lizzards', with foxes' tails twice as long. About their heads I only remember that their faces had an intelligent, human expression.

I saw them in a vast hall, big enough for them (given their size) to move about as in the open, and even in coaches. These coaches were in the grand style – state-coaches in fact – and advanced in a well ordered procession. It seemed to be a most solemn occasion. And the deportment of these creatures was ceremonial, and bore the imprint of a fine old civilization.

I talked with a few, and asked why I had never seen them before, or even heard of them. . . .

They answered that only the pure-in-heart were able to see them. In the mediaeval times the days of faith and candour, many had known them and conversed with them. (And I remembered at once how often, in those days, goblins, poltergeists, and the like had been mentioned). The sophisticated and sceptical eighteenth century (they went on) had declared they did not exist; no wonder if in consequence they had ceased to be met with.

But (said I) San Francesco d' Assisi, whose heart was no doubt of the purest – why had Saint Francis never mentioned them?

They answered: Saint Francis, pure in heart indeed, had actually seen them, but had thought their appearance to be a temptation – the Devil's doing – and therefore without reality. . .

That was my dream.

Trieste, 6 April, 1902.

Busoni

90

Interlude III:
Late Fauré

... Morel [the violinist] wanted to play bridge.... Madame Verdurin insisted on having 'a bit of violin playing' first. To everyone's surprise Monsieur de Charlus, who never said a word to anyone about his remarkable gifts, accompanied in perfect style, the last movement of Fauré's Piano and Violin Sonata – an agitated, restless Schumannesque piece, written, one should not forget, before Franck's sonata. And I felt that the Baron would pass on to Morel, beyond his virtuosity and his beautiful tone, the qualities of style and culture he stood most in need of.
Proust, *The Cities of the Plain*, II, chapter 2.

In these few lines Proust has given an accurate, almost an exhaustive description of one of Gabriel Fauré's most popular works: latterday romantic's music (Op. 13, 1876), in the manner of (and not as good as) Schumann's, made to be played by a young virtuoso violinist (even if somewhat raw) and a piano-playing aristocrat (even if a bit amateurish), and enjoyed in a *connoisseuse's* drawing-room. Moreover, Proust calls it 'the' Fauré Violin Sonata, disregarding the fact, as do nine dilettanti out of ten, even today, that the Second Violin Sonata (Op. 108) had been written, played and published in 1916. And yet even in the generally erratic progress of twentieth century music, I discover nothing as unexpected and almost bewildering as the meeting of these two items in the same composer's list. Aging composer's talent quite often deepens and expands: Verdi, Rimsky-Korsakov, Janáček and Frank Bridge have

91

been cases in point – after Beethoven. But Fauré is the one musician who at three-score-and-ten became a composer of another style, another language, another period and another rank.

The First Sonata, along with a good number of *nocturnes, valses caprices, barcarolles* and other piano works, had been derivative and facile: harmonically and melodically in the wake of Chopin – or Schumann, or Mendelssohn – with now and then a whiff of *Tristan* chromaticism. The Second Sonata is late Fauré and nothing else: strange, even austere melody, sustained (and often as though produced) by equally unconventional modal harmony, with a preference for the Lydian mode, which among all modes has the most unfamiliar, the least 'tonal' ring. (If you want to evoke the sound of late Fauré you have only to imagine or play the melodic clause of the downward second B, A, with the fifth F – C underneath.)

And to match this sort of modal harmony late Fauré's metrical patterns avoid symmetry and every sort of squareness.

The whole of Fauré's music written in his last decade – two Cello Sonatas, Second Piano Quintet, the Trio, his two last song cycles (*Mirages* and *L'Horizon Chimérique*), his *Fantaisie* for piano and orchestra, and his String Quartet, (completed in his eightieth year, a few weeks before his death in 1924) – is of this style: made of remoteness and a sort of dream-like unsentimental sadness, never misty but, on the contrary, very firmly and clearly drawn. Romantic drive and impetus may reappear – as in the last *Nocturne*, perhaps the most perfect and moving pages Fauré ever wrote. But it is romanticism revisited, wrapped in the intense melancholy of reminiscence, of *temps retrouvé*.

From a doubtless masterly nineteenth century *maître mineur* Fauré had turned into a *maître majeur* of unmistakably modern music. Maybe this fantastic metamorphosis was simply the response of a musician, whose originality and depth of imagination had been latent, to old age, deafness and ensuing disillusionment. Maybe he was unconsciously influenced by Debussy whom he did not like, and by his pupil Ravel of whose musical paradoxes and

ironies he did not approve; and it may be significant, too, that
Fauré was a church organist, and had in the sixties been educated,
not at the Conservatoire, but at Niedermeyer's École de Musique
Religieuse, a school that cultivated Gregorian modes and plainsong. He rose to fame, to be director of the Conservatoire (he was,
by the way, more efficient and enterprising than most) and a Grand
Officier in the *Légion d'Honneur*; to social prestige, thanks to his
irresistible feline charm; and to undisputed success, social and
academic, as a composer of elegant, virtuoso pieces, a Gounod-
esque *Requiem* and countless *romances* written for charming
hostesses. But all that was perhaps merely Fauré's triumphant yet
provisional progress, lasting forty years, on a path he had been
neither born nor brought up to tread.

It stands to reason that passages prefiguring late Fauré are found
in many of his earlier works, as in his 'lyrical tragedy' *Prometheus*
(1900) and his piano preludes, or his opera *Pénélope*, which –
undramatic and ill orchestrated though it is – opens his last group
of works (1913).

No wonder, on the other hand, that most of those who adored
their so delightfully mundane Fauré were sadly taken aback by his
lapse from conformism, and forthwith denounced it as a decrease
of vitality – just as most of the Forsytes would mark disapproval
and irritation, if, expecting to meet other Forsytes, they were
suddenly to face a set of characters out of *The Waves*.

Late Fauré means an interlude in the music of our time; and no
less arresting an interlude for having been without precedent, and
without sequel. Only a very thin thread links Fauré with Debussy,
who was a man of the aesthetic world of his day, attuned to
contemporary literature and painting. Fauré (indifferent, as no other
French composer ever was, to timbre and scoring) was in his later
works strictly and exclusively a technician of unworldly counterpoint. His pupils – Ravel, Kœchlin, Florent Schmitt – though they
admired him and proclaimed their gratitude, hardly ever followed
his example. Post-First-World-War composers did not like, respect
or even acknowledge Fauré's mastery any more than any other pre-
war composers' mastery. Not even the thinnest thread links late
Fauré with Vaughan Williams, the only composer who resembles
him in his lofty unostentatiousness and in having, in certain movements of his later symphonies, paradoxically combined (as did
Fauré in the astounding finale of his Second Quintet) the spirit of

static, archaic (and modern) modalism with the spirit of romantic development.

And if Britten favours the Lydian mode, it is not for having been influenced by Fauré, though this predilection may denote affinity, spiritual and musical, between the musician of the last song in *Winter Words* and the musician of *L'Horizon chimérique*.

Fauré

8 Rebellion against mastery: Les Six and Satie

By 1918 Oedipus complexes were rampant among the second generation of modern French musicians: it was no joke to be a composer with father-figures like Debussy, Ravel, Dukas and Roussel at one's back. In consequence a set of young musicians decided, or let their instinct decide for them, that – come what may – it should be a joke. A young poet, Jean Cocteau, was ready to define their doctrine – a doctrine each of them was free to accept or reject. For (in alphabetical order) Georges Auric, Louis Durey, Arthur Honegger, Darius Milhaud, Francis Poulenc, and Germaine Tailleferre formed 'not a school but a friendship'. A music critic of the period, H. Collet, wrote about 'les cinq Russes, les six Français et M. Erik Satie' in an article that provided the group with a name, a flattering precedent – the 'Mighty Five' – and an exemplary guide. Satie seemed to be judiciously chosen. Though born in 1866 he was no father-figure. 'Satie is difficult to worship,' said Cocteau. 'Not lending himself to deification is one of his charms.'

Satie

A fantastic, almost phantasmal figure, Satie had started in Wagnerian quarters, toyed with Sar Péladan's Rosicrucianism, and laid down the regulations and proclaimed himself the *Grand Parcier* of an imaginary company, modelled after the Order of the Holy Grail. The 'gothic' style of his script was very much like Baron Corvo's plus a touch of Albert Memorial, but the complexity of his decorative handwriting is delightfully contradicted by his unadorned music, which took its departure not from any neo-gothic or Wagne-

95

rian temple, but from a night club in Montmartre and from waltzes
written in the pure 1880 barrel-organ style. And then, quite un-
predictably again, Satie – as unobtrusive and as rebellious as
Debussy himself – came to anticipate essential Debussyisms.
Before Debussy nobody but Satie ever looked for this kind of cool,
non-psychological music. Several years ahead of *Pelléas*, Satie, who
never wrote an opera, suggested 'an orchestra that does not
grimace when one of the cast comes on stage. The trees painted on
the settings do not grimace either. Music considered as a decor. . . .'
And to write in this style Satie, exactly like Debussy later on,
resorted to archaic modes, static juxtaposition of chords and
parallel fifths and ninths.

Debussy neither denied nor ignored this affinity. His scoring of
two of Satie's three *Gymnopédies* makes genuine Satie as well as
genuine Debussy. And he inscribed a copy of his Baudelaire songs
'to Erik Satie, that mild and mediaeval musician who by mistake
entered the present century, just to please his true friend C. D.'
an inscription that echoes Satie's own, so admirably clear-
sighted statement : 'I was born very young, in an age that is very
old'.

With Satie anti-romanticism and anti-academicism, dislike of
pompousness and disapproval of every sort of overemphasis led,
beyond Debussy's *humour anglais* and French *gaminerie*, to favouring the ironically incongruous and the playfully absurd. As a
protest against impressionist, symbolist or other preciosities of
appellation he proposes *Flabby preludes for a dog* and *Desiccated
Embryos*. He was reproached with improvising his very short
pieces, and not caring overmuch about 'problems of form' – not
quite unjustly, for it needs a John Cage's super-Satie-ism to discover in Satie's music the sophisticated 'structural devices' of which
this composer was as innocent as Stravinsky was of the diverse
Hindu modes Messiaen analysed into *The Rite of Spring*. But Satie
promptly retorted by naming his next set of pieces *Morceaux en
forme de poire*. Between the staves of his music, he indicated how
it should be played – and rarely forgot to choose remarkably un-
informative directions, such as 'Consider with great care' or (in a
piece called *The Disgusted Beau* III) 'His legs, he is very proud of
them'; or in Latin *Substantialis*.

His writings with no music involved – mock manifestos, letters,
apophthegms – are of the same vein. 'Do smoke, my boy, for if you

don't, somebody else will smoke in your stead.' Or, to wind up a description of his workaday manner of living: 'Every evening my valet takes my temperature, and gives me another one. . . .'

Erik Leslie Satie, born (1866) in Honfleur, was the son of a Norman father and a Scottish mother. (Pawkiness accounted for.) His early musical training, at the Conservatoire was half-hearted and perfunctory. His piano teacher advised him to join a harmony class; the professor of harmony declared he had better play the piano. Much later, by 1905 and long after having produced some of his best work, he resumed his studies and entered Roussel's counterpoint class at the Schola Cantorum, won his diploma and made fun of his official consecration as a *contrapontiste*. Which proves that he knew pretty well that conventional schooling, if it adds academicism to academicists' scores, makes rebels' scores more effectively rebellious. Likewise his reiterated and ludicrously ill-timed attempts to enter the Institut de France, as Guiraud's or Ambroise Thomas's successor, were not a mere *blague*. In Satie's music nine bars out of ten are homely and simple; in the tenth an element of mild incongruity and ambiguous naïvety throws a different light on the whole period's meaning. Not unlike the Douanier Rousseau's and Lewis Carroll's, Satie's charm is very much the charm of a child that has decided to be an *enfant terrible* in order to assuage its terror of having lost its way in a *selva oscura*. The necessity of 'building one's personal raft' (Herbert Read again: see page 74) and renouncing any public conveyance is essentially a melancholy and toilsome affair. Let us try to make it less disheartening by shaping our rafts into portmanteau vehicles – as Lewis Carroll might call them – rafts preposterously rigged out with elusive oars, prow figures and sails that will faintly remind the imaginative onlooker of Viking prows, galleon's square sails, and trireme's oars, conjured up in a Victorian magic lantern.

Satie is unique, and endearing. The sketchy musical short stories he used to write have the flavour of genuine fairy-tales. With an unassuming *recitativo* sustained by sparse common chords, his *Death of Socrates* is no less moving than Monteverde's death of Seneca, and Debussy's death of Mélisande. Yet Satie is no match for Debussy: the Bellman's wisdom is not Prospero's. Serious or jocose, written before or after, Satie's pieces are inchoate prefigurations or shadowy echos of Debussy's. Even *Parade* (1916), with its Picasso settings, is – in spite of its lottery-wheel, its typewriters and other unexpected percussion – a second version, diluted rather than aggrandized, of *La Serenade interrompue*. Nevertheless we would not dispense with snark-hunting Satie. Without him twentieth century music would be as incomplete as a fancy fair without a lottery-wheel.

His life, like most consistent humorists', was all dignity and frustration. After retiring to Arcueil, a gloomy suburb south of Paris, he supervised some sort of musical kindergarten, which was so much appreciated that the order of the Palmes académiques (generally granted to aging schoolmasters) was conferred upon him. Between Satie and every single one of his many friends quarrels arose 'as everyone knows' – because somebody had taken his facetiousness too seriously; or not seriously enough; or because he suspected somebody to have pinched his umbrella. Admired by Debussy, Ravel, Braque, Derain, Picasso and Picabia, he was miserably poor. He felt comforted no doubt when hailed by Les Six and worshipped by a few pupils, who styled themselves École d'Arcueil. Yet he was as sceptical about Satie influence and the Satie school as Debussy had been about Debussy followers. And he was no less sceptical about any sort of human relationship. Asked by his sister-in-law why he had never married, he answered : 'Because I could never have appeared as a married man without re-appearing as a cuckold'.

After his death (1925) Milhaud discovered in his squalid hotel room half a dozen velvet suits all alike, some spinsterishly impeccable linen and, behind the piano, two manuscript scores Satie had more than once sadly mentioned as having been left on a bus somewhere between Paris and Arcueil.

With Les Six Satie's scepticism about a Satie school proved less unreasonable than Cocteau's confidence. Contrary to what Cocteau said, they would have done better to have taken Satie for a god than for a master. Douanier Rousseau followers and Lewis Carroll followers would hardly be well advised painters or poets. Moreover Les Six did not resemble Satie. They were neither 'mild' nor 'mediaeval', and it was not in the least by mistake that they had entered the twentieth century. They were well-to-do, matter-of-fact and down-to-earth. 'A dreamer is always a bad poet' said Cocteau, implying that not to dream, or at least to ignore one's dreams, is the first step towards being a good musician. In other words beware of dreaming and avoid being troubled by apparitions in the form of father-figures: 'No more clouds, waves, aquariums and mermaids; enough of fragrance-of-the-night music. We want our music to settle on solid ground. We need everyday's music . . . not music that rocks like a hammock, but music built like a house to live in . . . Music is not always a gondola, a race-horse or a tight rope; music is also, at times, a stool or a chair.'

The idea of *musique d'ameublement* was in fact Satie's, and music considered as furniture meant going one better than music considered as décor. For we look at décor, but let our 'everyday' furniture surround us unnoticed. And it made no odds that Satie had not quite succeeded when he first presented this music to be heard but not listened to, with a piano, three clarinets and a trombone posted on several sides of the hall. In spite of Satie's entreaties – 'Mais parlez! Mais parlez donc!' – the public had refused to give the required disrespect and inattention.

Satie's *musique d'ameublement* meant a farcical protest against the romantic's exigency of rapt attention and his emphatic habit of listening, face buried in palms. Unwittingly perhaps, he suggested a return to the ways of the Italian opera-goers of Stendhal's times. Les Six were looking for something different with their musical furniture: not so much for their public's aloofness as for their own. A comfortable chair to sit on provides a vantage point for exorcizing the father-images. Debussy, Ravel and Dukas, makers of music haunted by mermaids and unsubstantial fragrance, had never shunned the discomfort of their quest for perfection. Encouraged by Cocteau, Les Six, *pour changer tout cela,* were going to be the carefree musical carpenters and cabinet-makers of an industrial age, who, since even craftsman's mastery and perfection seem to be outdated niceties, were rather proud of their expeditious hand-to-mouth methods.

In 1920 Les Six – five of them, Durey being absent – wrote collectively for the Ballets Suédois company *Les Mariés de la Tour Eiffel* to a libretto by Cocteau. A ballet intended to be modern, on the surrealist side: actors turned into gramophones, and instead of the familiar little bird, an ostrich was released from the Press photographer's camera; telegrams appeared in the guise of winged beings; the General has scarcely spoken at the wedding – 'and so beautifully, with an intelligence far above his rank' – when he is devoured by the lion he mistook for a mirage. The music was intended to be modern in the French and nothing-but-French manner, untainted by Teutonic and romantic influence, and – in contrast to *Pelléas* and *Daphnis et Chloé* – untainted by Slavism. And these moderately ambitious intentions resulted in a score that is very modest and quite pleasant, sounds like Offenbach spiced with a modicum of wrong notes, and does not pretend to excel the ephemeral value of the show it accompanies. And both music and show dwindle into complete insignificance when compared with theatrical fantasies that have dramatic shape and musical style – like *L'Histoire du Soldat* or *Arlecchino*, both written at about the same time.

Among Les Six, Arthur Honegger, though born (1892) at Le Havre, need not be portrayed in this essay. As a Swiss and as the first remarkable Swiss composer after Schnyder von Wartensee (1786–1868), he was partly spared his French friends' sensitivity to the overwhelming prestige of the great French composers. He was a born master and a very robust, and accomplished, if somewhat pedestrian, one.

Auric, Durey and Tailleferre

Georges Auric entered the musical scene at fifteen (1914), with *Interludes*, a set of melodies. A certain technical clumsiness adds to the modern chic of his early scores. But he soon evolved into a most competent composer of ballet music, beginning with *Les Fâcheux* (1923). It was music in the *musique d'ameublement* fashion, apt to provide choreographers with musical furniture as remarkable for its lightness as its solidity. A *belle époque* waltz he wrote for a film about Toulouse-Lautrec won him greater success, in the way of performing rights and recordings for instruments of every description, than any of his contemporaries ever met with – a fluke he acknowledged with his well known sense of humour and that natural modesty he often chooses to disguise under a mask of assurance. For some years head of the Paris Opéra, he was enterprising enough to entrust Pierre Boulez with the direction of the first French performance of *Wozzeck*.

Louis Durey and Germaine Tailleferre are composers of technically unexceptionable scores that are neither too long nor too short, never too serious, never frivolous. Revisited today their music seems to have been written rather by respectful followers of Debussy, Ravel or Fauré than by anti-impressionist rebels. In the republic of twentieth-century muscians they rank as excellent but in no wise prominent citizens.

Milhaud

Darius Milhaud's prominence on the contrary is undisputed. His *œuvre* defeats, by sheer bulk, any attempt at overlooking or belittling its significance. By 1961, when he was sixty-nine, his catalogue reached up to Op. 401. I doubt whether any musician or music-lover exists who knows the whole of Milhaud the composer. And I think it equally improbable that Milhaud the man could ever have been disliked by anybody. I hardly ever met a musician as exempt from every trace of pettiness or as benevolent and urbane – and courageous: an incurable glandular deficiency has made him permanently a partial invalid, a fate he has accepted – nay, seems to ignore – with smiling stoicism.

He comes from a Jewish family established in Provence, since the fifteenth century according to traceable tradition, or before Herod, as the legend goes. His great-grandfather, picturesquely named Benestrue Milhaud, helped Mirabeau to 'go North' and start his career in Paris: Darius has good extra-musical reasons to be artistocratically debonair. And if, as a composer, the father-figures ever threatened his equanimity, this threat was soon overcome by means of a triumphant superiority complex. With him self-confidence has never been a mask or an attitude, or even second nature. It is an inborn certitude. When he felt unable to learn the rules of Conservatoire-taught harmony, he did not decide – like other rebels – to relish breaking the rules; he simply decided to ignore them altogether. They did not suit him, *ergo* they were perfectly useless and as good as non-existent.

His encounter and ensuing association with Paul Claudel, whose secretary and whose musician he became in 1917, no doubt reinforced this frame of mind. For Claudel, a strong personality and a great and already famous poet, was apt to influence Milhaud, being his senior by twenty-four years. And Claudel was candidly convinced that every line written by himself was dictated by the purest spirit of poetry, and more often than not by the Holy Ghost.

It was easy for Milhaud to interpret the situation of music as it suited him. The aftermath of romanticism had done away with the last taboos of forbidden dissonance and tonal command. (Milhaud, who was the first to conduct *Pierrot Lunaire* in France, knew everything about Viennese atonalism.) On the other hand, and in the other camp, Debussy had shown that music's vividness and immediacy could not be regained unless the principle of development, overworked for a hundred years, gave way to the 'static principle' of juxtaposition. In consequence, by 1918 nothing would prevent a composer from piling up any amount of dissonance, and then setting side by side any number of vertical chance encounters. Nevertheless this sort of enfranchised music, still apt to shock the general public, was not yet taken for granted, but welcomed as pleasurably non-conformist by advanced listeners.

Thus Milhaud's music, by definition militant though in fact extremely relaxed, appeared as highly challenging and explosive to friend and foe alike. At the first performance of his *Études* for piano and orchestra (1921) the doorkeeper of the Salle Gaveau was seen calling in a policeman to protect the composer, for the turmoil of aggressive sound from the platform was echoed in the hall by a turmoil of frenzied protest and counter-protest. These *Études* remain indeed, even today, one of Milhaud's most striking works. Though conscientiously and elaborately written out – even fugue-writing occurs – it sounds, surprisingly and quite excitingly like one of today's partially improvised 'open forms': clash-counter-clash instead of point-counter-point.

André Malraux has said, not long ago, that (in contrast with other French writers, such as André Gide) 'he cares, and always has cared, for creation rather than for perfection'. So does Milhaud, and his musical vitality never shrinks from taking arbitrary sound and ramshackle construction in its stride. And Milhaud's youthful eagerness and pleasure when putting minims, crochets and quavers together is often infectious. His music (1914–22) to Claudel's translation of Aeschylos, even apart from its scenes for speaking chorus (then an impressive novelty), retains even in 1974 a good deal of its barbaric impact. *L'Homme et son désir* was written in Brazil in 1921, and the spell of its virgin-forest-like entanglements of tropical drumming and voodoo melody has not faded. The jazz-inspired *La Création du Monde* anticipated in 1923, and later on recalled, *Green Pastures* and its charm. *Le Bœuf sur le toit* (1919), much in the same style, was destined to survive thanks to the popularity and the prestige of its godchild – a Paris night club of the same name.

Not a few other early works of Milhaud's are pleasant, beyond their youthfulness and *beauté du diable*, for his straightforward handling of polytonality – a device, occasionally proposed earlier (with due sophistication) by Debussy and by Stravinsky. But with Milhaud it makes *Saudades do Brazil* (1921) or the canonic section of his Second Violin Sonata (1917), sound like some Brahms *Charaktertanz* gone wrong or a Bach invention revised by the naughty little girl who has run away from Dr Gradus at Parnassus's lessons.

Even at his noisiest Milhaud is never pompous, and bad taste is never among the faults of even his faultiest score. In 1954 he scored a terrifying text about Buchenwald and Auschwitz (by the French-Catalan poet Jean Cassou) into a short cantata of admirable dignity and expressive restraint (*Le Château de feu*). Disarming (if not redeeming) qualities of good taste and good faith, discretion and sincerity, stand out even in his most unaccountable undertakings, such as the setting of Pope John xxIII's encyclical *Pacem in terris*.

Milhaud has written – one is tempted to say 'has, of course, written' – several *grands opéras* and several short operas – and several very short operas (*opéras minutes*). *Maximilien* (1930) and *Bolivar* (1943) are each a loosely interlinked set of scenes – some more, some less singable; some operatically effective, others not. It would have needed at least a Mussorgsky to make them as convincing as the tragedy *Maximilien* and the epic *Bolivar* are meant to be. The libretti of his short operas *Les Malheurs d'Orphée* (1924) and *Le pauvre Matelot* (1926) have poetic atmosphere and intensity. In the music, too, there is something to move susceptible listeners: Milhaud's biographer Paul Collaer, a remarkable musician and a sensitive observer, extols the quiver of both the singing and the orchestral playing in *Le pauvre Matelot*, and cites a passage from *Orphée* as being 'of an impressive *absolue nudité* hardly equalled in contemporary music'. Other listeners, I am afraid, cannot help feeling that this music, though indeed *molto simpatica*, lets them down for being weak of spine and vague of contour – sketched and drafted rather than carried through.

Milhaud symphonies, Milhaud concertos, Milhaud chamber music: score piled upon score, and in every single one of them needles of musical gold to be looked for in long rows of bottles of musical hay. And all of them composed by a musician who, like Hindemith, according to Constant Lambert, '... seems to think

H

that some mystic value resides in the mere performance of notes – that the scraping of horsehair over catgut is in itself a health-giving and praiseworthy action. . . .'

His String Quartets Nos 14 and 15 are devised to be played either separately or simultaneously as an octet. We are at once reminded of a similar *tour de force* in Bach's *Kunst der Fuge*. With Bach it was the triumph of geometry and music combined; it was a musician's humility and confidence in praising God framed into a composer's pride and counterpoint. With Milhaud it means nondescript impulse framed into indifferent design: let four or eight fiddlers fiddle away, let happy-go-lucky lines cross and uncross; and let it be God's business to pick and choose, as the old Crusader suggested.

Poulenc

Like Milhaud, Francis Poulenc (1899–1963) was always an improviser. Unlike Milhaud, who improvises pencil in hand, Poulenc improvised his compositions on his piano, and his excellent piano-playing made him prey to all the mercilessly traditionalist formulas and reflexes of the keyboard. In sharpest contrast to Milhaud's unkempt and negligent originality Poulenc is always naïvely and shamelessly unoriginal. His swift fingers, obeying the keys' injunctions, seem to be incessantly quoting. Nothing to do with Ravel's or Stravinsky's taking to imitation as the starting-point of a dialogue with the past (see page 27), Poulenc lets the past speak alone, without adding a word, and proposes bald pastiche. Mozart, Chabrier-cum-Gounod, Italianate Liszt, Ravel, Debussy (preferably the Debussy of the *Arabesques*), Stravinsky (preferably *Pulcinella* or *Apollon Musagète*) – Poulenc will string them together like so many scintillating parti-coloured beads that are often adroitly matched, and just as often oddly ill-assorted. In this manner his popular Chabrier-cum-Ravel-inspired Toccata leads up to some other and unforeseen quotation; and his brilliant and most effective *Concert champêtre* for harpsichord and orchestra is probably the wildest medley of styles any composer ever dared to offer.

No wonder that he has met with great and unflagging success. Original and often aggressively dissonant, modern musicians are feared by many like big bad wolves. And even those favouring 'enfranchised consonance' – Satie, for example, an indomitable

artist disguised as a *farceur* – were, not without reason, suspected
of being wolves in sheep's clothing. But Poulenc, an extremely
intelligent, highly gifted and wholly unaggressive sheep in amusing
and picturesque harlequin's clothing, therefore seemed to deserve a
welcome with triple flourish.

The 1920s were a decade when, as Aldous Huxley remarked in
Two or Three Graces, 'modern' and 'eighteenth century' tended
towards synonymity – at least in certain quarters. And Poulenc was
indeed a mixture of Huxley's Clegg and an *abbé de Cour.* He was
also a diplomatic and open-minded lion in every fashionable salon
who would accompany with perfection and ease and true
eighteenth century aloofness, romantic lieder, or Debussy, or his
own Gounod-esque, Debussyian, Chabrier-esque or (unwillingly)
Fauré-esque *mélodies,* sung by Pierre Bernac, one of the rare
unexceptionable musicians among singers. Poulenc *mélodies* are
always remarkably well-balanced duets for voice and instrument,
and they are, moreover – perhaps for their gusto and easy blending
of borrowed material – endowed with the unquestionable Poulenc
charm, never questioned because near-irresistible.

Poulenc was also very much *du côté de Guermantes* when
talking with sincere and becoming modesty about his own music,
and with the same sincerity and with unenvious benevolence,
about other musicians'. Proust's Duchesse would have delighted in
his anti-pedantic contempt of consistency in matters of taste and
opinion. Naturally enough he adored Mozart. He also adored
Richard Strauss. He was bored by Wagner though he admired him
(or contrariwise). It stands to reason that he felt little affinity with
rigorous musical architects like Roussel or Dukas; yet to prefer
Charpentier's *Louise* (that monument of vulgarity) to *Ariane et
Barbe Bleu* is going to extremes, and even beyond. He liked Bach's
Preludes and Fugues, as played (and romanticized) by Landowska,
met the *Brandenburg* Concertos 'with veneration and indifference',
but would for nothing in the world have dispensed with Beethoven's quartets, 'which are an incessant discovery'. It is curious
how little such discoveries influenced Poulenc the composer. But it
is much curiouser still – as Alice would say – that the only music he
dismisses with uncompromising harshness should have been
Fauré's *Requiem* – probably the work that comes nearest to
Poulenc's own music, and sounds like Poulenc at his very best.

His vocal music is indeed his best, and especially his *a cappella* music – sacred or secular. More than in most other forms of composition there has been, through four or five centuries, an unbroken continuity of style in *a cappella* writing – and even a tradition of archaism – and Poulenc's compositions in this genre are, for once, not *pastiches* but simply true to tradition. His choral pieces are all pleasant melody and elegant harmony, polyphony being hardly ever resorted to. And a good number of discreet musical cameos have been the result, such as *Sept chansons* (1936), *Un Soir de neige* (1944), *Figure humaine* (1934), *and the Mass in G* (1937).

After two ballets – *Les Biches* (1923) and *Les Animaux modèles* (1943) – Poulenc wrote three operas. *Les Mamelles de Tirésias* (1944) is an Offenbachish affair, akin to *Les Mariés de la Tour Eiffel*, with a brilliant role for a high soprano. The text is a farce, improvised by Apollinaire, about the reprehensible practice of birth control in pre-war France. The music is brisk and amusing – though a much earlier work of Poulenc's on poems by Apollinaire is better: *Le Bestiaire*, a set of short pieces for voice and piano (1919), is witty, unpretentious and almost perfect, as are the contemporary *Mouvements perpétuels* for piano solo. Poulenc, too, was one of the *beauté du diable* composers.

In his other two operas Poulenc turned – for style if not for idiom – from Offenbach to Puccini, an evolution that was not a mark of progress. Yet *verismo* was not out of place in a maudlin monodrama by Cocteau about a luckless girl who, alone in her room, accepts with despair and heroism the cowardly adieu addressed to her over the telephone by her lover. Denise Duval, an excellent singer and a fascinating actress, has made *La Voixe Humaine* (1958) a triumph.

Les Dialogues des Carmélites (1956) is quite another matter. It is based upon a film script by Bernanos after Gertrud von Lefort's story: the terrifying and admirable tragedy of a young girl's fear of fate, of life, of everything – an irrational and insuperable fear, eventually overcome through the mystery, almost through the miracle, of faith – under circumstances that would have defeated the fearless, and did in fact defeat one of them. With Poulenc this tragedy is turned into nothing better than a cruel show, set to very temperate, modern eighteenth century music, about the horrors of *l'année terrible*, 1793. Musical characterization is not even attempted: hardboiled man of the world, naïve youngster, Mother-Superior of a convent or valet – they all express themselves in the same tepid sort of *recitativo arioso.* In the last act the drama comes to life and culminates, Tosca-fashion, in the gruesome reiterated click of the guillotine. Well written for voices, transparently and sparingly scored, easy to listen to, or to daydream to, *Les Dialogues des Carmélites* is as many an opera-lover wants his beloved opera to be, and was hailed as Poulenc's *chef d'œuvre.* It did not, however, re-enter the repertoire of the Paris Opera under the directorship of Poulenc's friend Auric.

Though a sincere and devout Roman Catholic, Poulenc was ill equipped to deal, as a musician, with Kierkegaardian or Bernanosian problems, or for that matter with any problems. He was typically French – according to those, mainly outside France, who forget that Bernanos and Georges de La Tour are just as French as Maupassant and Quentin Latour, and define the French character in terms of lightness, practical rationalism and refined sensuousness, a Dufy's sense of elegance, an acute vision of the foreground of things and little patience with those who let themselves be attracted by the uncomfortable depth of the background. Along such lines of definition Poulenc has been rashly compared to Dufy: the twenties were inclined to efface the differences between sense of style and mere charm of mannerism, and between consummate skill and dazzling half-amateurish facility. Poulenc, the puckish charmer among Les Six, was not a Dufy: no more than the puckish inspirer of Les Six, Cocteau – though an arresting draughtsman, and one who knew a few things about the decoration of sanctuaries – was a Matisse or a Caplet.

Poulenc

9 Towards Avantgarde 1: Jeune France

As it happened, four other young composers were going to propound in 1935 quite a different sort of musical Frenchness. 'Jeune France', said the manifesto issued by Yves Baudrier, André Jolivet, Daniel Lesur and Olivier Messiaen, 'takes its name from a similar movement initiated by Berlioz. Conditions of life are ever hardening and tend more and more toward the impersonal and the mechanical. Music, therefore, should unwaveringly follow the opposite path – the path of spiritual generosity and violence . . . We want our music to be young and unhampered, free from clichés, whether academic or revolutionary.' In other words no 'eighteenth-century modernism', no drawing-roomishness, no aloofishness, no worldly-wise ironies. Rather a streak of the neo-gothic, and of back-to-romanticism.

Not unlike Les Six, however, the four Jeune France are a heterogeneous batch. 'Spiritual violence' and contempt of academicism are not among Daniel Lesur's (born 1908) main traits. A church organist, teacher of counterpoint at the Schola Cantorum, and later on an efficient controller of television music, he wrote orchestral and chamber works: *Suite française* (1935), *Variations* for piano and strings (1943), *Suite mediévale* (1949), *Festival Overture* (1951). These scores are always elegant in manner, often modal, sometimes monodic, on occasions impressionist, and regularly provided with a modicum of dissonance – wrong notes added, not, as by Les Six, for fun, but in all seriousness to eschew the reproach and the danger of submissiveness to 'academic cliché'. A well-proportioned and by no means over-erotic *a cappella* version of the *Song of Songs* dates from 1952. More recently his opera *Andrea del Sarto* was awarded the Prix de la Ville de Paris and produced in Marseilles, Toulouse, and Rouen. Its style is discreetly Wagnerized and less discreetly sentimentalized *Pelléas,* and its libretto, after Alfred de Musset (in 1830 the Jeune France poet *par excellence*), a variation on the *Tristan* theme: the lovers prefer eloping to *Liebestod,* and it is Marke who takes the deadly potion; but not before having sent word to the fugitives, to spare them undignified and unnecessary haste of flight.

Baudrier

Born 1906, Yves Baudrier, a lean, bright-eyed, hollow-cheeked Celt, bird-of-prey's nose and good Samaritan's smile, is romantic as romantic can be in that he contrives to stamp his endearing personality upon every page of music he writes – a much rarer merit in our 'mechanical and impersonal' day than in Schumann's. And it is indeed an uncommon experience to meet with Baudrier's settings of verse by Tristan Corbière (that equally Celtic and haunted *poète maudit*), his orchestral fantasies *Raz de Sein* and *Le Musicien dan la cité* or his *Credo, Adjuva incredulitatem meam* for voices and orchestra. His is music whose childlike vividness and directness makes us forget to ask questions about their style and technique. It needs an afterthought and a second hearing to notice that there are shaky spots in his more extended pieces, and to wonder about his being at once a romantic and a Debussyist. He escapes, thanks to Debussy's intercession, the spuriousness and pomposity of the post-romantic and, by the grace of romanticism's immediacy, escapes the staleness of Debussy imitation.

As a composer of film music Baudrier has never been surpassed by any I know of. His music has turned more than one film into a better work of art. The sombre anxiety and determination of *La Bataille du Rail* (a film about the Resistance) is mirrored and deepened by Baudrier's tempo and rhythms, down to the rhythm of awareness and hesitancy in the face of the inescapable, illustrated by the *ostinato* of a leaking tap. Again, in *Le Tempestaire,* a film about the survival of crystal-gazing and other magical practices in Brittany, Baudrier's (maybe Celtic) sense of the numinous confers on a documentary the rank of an opera ballet: the music comes in to express the supernatural – according to Busoni, one of music's few operatic callings.

Jolivet

In the Jeune France group, André Jolivet, born in Paris (1905), has no doubt been the driving power. Beside the elegant Lesur and the unwordly Baudrier he represented a coarser grain. Unromantically a craftsman, but a romantically picturesque one, square of jaw and strong of fist, he is ready to prove a hewer of rough and unwieldy chunks of sound in the backwoods of music. And whereas so many others did not carry their time-travelling farther than such highly civilized stations as the eighteenth century or that mediaeval frontier between Gregorian modes and C major, Jolivet set out for the prehistorical regions of *Ur-Musik*, when singing, piping and drumming did not mean cadence and sonata, but the evocation or the driving away of demons and other spirits. He had never a greater wish than to be on intimate terms with the primaeval musical magic that musical rationalism – renaissance, eighteenth-century or other – had done its best to hold at arm's length or ignore. (See Busoni's dream.)

But before starting upon his expedition, young Jolivet had been advised by his teacher Paul Le Flem, an exceptionally clear-sighted musician, to take counsel of the only guide to the musical antipodes then available: Edgard Varèse. Varèse's scores were in those days (early thirties) listened to and commented upon as 'absurd, neither head nor tail' or, at best 'quite interesting; not "music", of course'. Many scores, since Monteverde's had been thus welcomed, with little variety in the terms employed. But with Varèse such reactions were a little less unjustified than before. For Varèse's was an attempt of breathtaking boldness at getting away not only from 'academic clichés' but from every wonted tonal or modal connotation of harmony and melody. And even from the instruments' expressive connotations; Varèse's drums, trumpets, flutes and violins are no longer as Haydn as well as Debussy and Schoenberg took them for granted: warlike, pastoral or sensuously eloquent. They are, all of them, called up to partake in what might be called musically non-representational experiments in sound and rhythm. This was a break with History of Music's continuity which it was not too far fetched to call a return to *Ur-Musik,* straight from musical Pegasus's magical mouth.

Varèse had never written for the piano, and his reasonably astute disciple Jolivet decided that his suite *Mana* should be Varèsian piano music. 'Mana' signifies the current of magic force that circulates between man and his 'familiar fetishes', and these six short studies were inspired by half a dozen figurines of wire, wood and wool to be found on the composer's mantelpiece, and representing a goat, a cow, a little copper Punchinello, the Princess of Bali, a bird of paradise and winged Pegasus. And *Mana,* composed in 1935, has in 1974 lost nothing of the challenging avantgarde modernism that inhabits its strange, haunting, tuneless melodic lines, the tension of its rhythmic asymmetry and pitiless dissonance. *Mana's* Minor 9ths and Augmented 4ths go beyond disobeying the academic rules that would order them to be resolved: they are not even content with remaining pointedly unresolved as are the dissonances of Viennese atonalism. They are bone and flesh of a sort of musical conglomerate radiating multiple sound that no more calls for resolution than does the rustle of leaves, the clangour of hammer on anvil, or the growl of axe-smitten trees.

A few other works of Jolivet's have been written in the same spirit as *Mana*: *Five Incantations* for solo flute (1936) *Danses rituelles* for solo piano or orchestra (1939); also his String Quartet (1934), especially its slow movement, subsequently transcribed for string orchestra. Among his later scores some are so incredibly tame and conventional that one would hesitate to ascribe them to the same André Jolivet. Others again – like his Piano Concerto (1950) with its somewhat belated *Rite-of-Spring* reminiscences, his symphonies, his *Suite transocéane,* his piano sonatas and several concertos with chamber orchestra – are remarkable for their mastery, eloquence and energy. Yet there is always something domesticated and professional about their intended avantgardism. Music-as-magic is still aimed at, and the symbols in the sounds of lightning and fire evoke, as of old, the wrath of the weather-gods, and Phœnix, that wonderful bird. But not without an afterthought about Benjamin Franklin and Phœnix Ltd, the dependable insurance company. To do André Jolivet justice we have to think of him, and to champion him, first and last, as the composer of *Mana.*

Messiaen

Olivier Messiaen's mother was a poetess, his father a professor of English. The poetess, when pregnant, would immortalize the event:

> Child, pale embryo, thou sleepest in the waters
> Like a dead little god in a coffin of glass.
> Thine, through these early days, is the enjoyable weightless
> existence
> Of fish slumbering under the reeds. . . .

Nine years later in his father's library he read Shakespeare and Tennyson (in romantically illustrated translations), and tried his wholly untutored hand at composing a musical portrait of *The Lady of Shallott*. All this was very promising, and so were his beginnings as a professional musician. He won prizes at the Paris Conservatoire, in Dukas', Maurice Emmanuel's and Marcel Dupré's classes. At twenty-two he was the youngest appointed church organist in France. His first compositions, however, are quite unadventurous. And, rather suddenly, probably after meeting André Jolivet, he decided that a composer born in 1908 should go farther afield than his well written Debussyist piano preludes (1929) or his even better written but rather scholastic *Variations* for violin and piano (1932).

By 1944 he had written several scores in a new style, such as the *Quatuor pour le fin du temps, Visions de l'Amen* (for two pianos), *Trois petites liturgies de la Présence divine* (female voice and instruments) and *Vingt regards sur L'Enfant Jésus* – all of them inspired by his strong and emphatically proclaimed Roman Catholic faith, and written in a conspicuously avantgarde idiom. In the same year he published *The Technique of my Musical Language*, a curious textbook meant to lay down in full detail, his methods 'as far as rhythm, melody and harmony are concerned', *viz*, to describe the rational substructure of his music – music intended to be unceasingly and almost mediaevally spiritual, but in fact quite often sensual and sentimental in the post-romantic manner, with motives à la Scriabin and à la Chausson rather incongruously embedded in a 'liturgical' context.

'As far as Rhythm is concerned. . . .' In his first chapters Messiaen, perhaps unwittingly, goes quite far towards explaining his strange way of composing. The word 'rhythm' occurs every second

line, but the notion in hand is exclusively 'metre'. To composers
with rhythmic imagination – the composer of *Mana*, for instance, in
Messiaen's immediate neighbourhood – metre is simply a question
of notation: rhythmic tension, and rhythmic impulses have to be
written out, exactly or approximately ((*rubato*) in terms of minims,
crotchets, quavers, triplets, syncopes etc. Messiaen tries, the other
way round, to build up his rhythm out of metrical patterns – sets of
3+2+5+7 quavers or the like – later on to be varied and developed by 'dots added' or 'dots suppressed', i.e. 3 quavers+5 semiquavers, or 3 quavers+3 semiquavers instead of 3+2 quavers.
Examples are given, and he describes one of them (from his
Quatuor) as 'an irresistible movement of steel' and 'a formidable
granite of sound'. But it appears that the passage in question,
whatever its merits, is nothing less than rhythmically enhanced by
the 'dot-values', systematically added or taken away every now and
then, which merely seem to replace a live *rubato* by an arithmeti-
cally rationalized one, its rhythmical drive being stifled in the
process.

As though feeling that he has somehow to make up for the
dullness of this mechanical procedure, Messiaen refers to non-
symmetrical Hindu metres (which very probably represent live
rhythm in actual Hindu music, but *in abstracto* represent nothing
of the sort); and then introduces the fanciful notion of '*the charm of
impossibilities*'. A fanciful notion indeed: for if patterns like
2+3+2 do not allow of a retrograde form – being identical whether
read from left to right or from right to left – that 'impossibility' may
have a slight technical bearing upon a *canon cancrizans*. But not
one musician in a hundred will feel inclined to endow so prosaic a
point of syntax with any sort of charm.

'As far as melody and harmony are concerned' Messiaen recommends faraway harmonics (e.g. F sharp in relation to C), plainsong,
Hindu modes and other modes, polymodalism and atonalism, and
recourse to models found in ancient and modern masters' scores,
and gives examples of what happens to passages of Debussy's or
Ravel's, when filtered 'through the distorting prism of my technique'. (Once more we are reminded of Ravel's and Stravinsky's
dialogues with the History of Music, but Ravel and Stravinsky
converse with their foregoers' music and style, Messiaen with their
notes and finger-prints.) He also recommends and exemplifies
'clusters of chords' and 'rainbows'; and, with special emphasis, his

beloved bird-song, materialized through high-pitched loquacious up-and-down arabesques, staccatos adorned with grace-notes, trills etc.

In practice Messiaen's compositions are much less varied than one would expect from his theory, from his fabulous memory and his dyed-in-the-wool musicianship (I never met with more sensitive and colourful a pianist), and from his familiarity with music of every sort and period, which makes him so accomplished and versatile a teacher. Again and again he seems to refer to one model, not mentioned in *Technique de mon Langage*, but known to every concert-goer:

from Chopin's Third Scherzo

– a model that contains the two main colours of Messiaen's palette, the two main elements of his style: dark hymn-tune melody and harmony on one side and an iridescence of twitterings and tintinnabulations on the other.

Messiaen as a composer is a poor rhythmist, and hardly a better polyphonist. His ingenuity in handling his 'distorting prism' and in concocting synthetic melody and harmony, however, is never at a loss, and his art of linking chord with chord truly admirable. He shrewdly blends the reassuringly facile with the exquisitely far-fetched. He also knows everything about the spell of relentless repetition, blunt *ostinato* and blunt contrasts, and rightly trusts their hypnotic virtue when using them as a substitute for musical architecture. On the other hand, his inventiveness in flavouring his productions with comments, edifying or picturesque, or preferably both, is boundless. But when, in *Catalogue d'Oiseaux* (how much longer than Leporello's catalogue of girls!), flocks of birds with never-heard-of names are summoned up – birds whose almost indistinguishable differences of chirping it would demand squads of ornithologists to spot – or when (*The Transfiguration of Christ*,

114

1968) he declares that, to the words *This is my beloved Son*, his music is going to symbolize first 'sonship with a capital S' and then 'sonship with a small s', such by-products of a composer's ambition cannot be written off as just exuberance of imagination and poetic fancy.

They are plain mumbo-jumbo – the same mumbo-jumbo resorted to by the music itself when (in *Et exspecto resurrectionem mortuorum*, 1965) challenging, aggressive chords alternate with a very homely, if not particularly well-shaped, unison in the low woodwind, and with the cheapest sort of ominous tam-tam soli; or when (in *The Transfiguration* again) we are invited to hear, in a wholly uncongenial context, a sweet solo for cello – as if the composer had sworn to make avantgarde music palatable for Puccini lovers.

Small wonder that his success has been widespread and lasting.

Messiaen

10 Towards Avantgarde II: Dallapiccola and Petrassi

It stands to reason that by 1925 Italian composers felt less intimidated at being 'second generation' than did their French contemporaries. In Rome and Florence Casella, Malipiero, and even Busoni and Debussy were looked upon as encouraging godfather-figures rather than awesome father-figures. And, quite unintimidated, two young rivals set out to pour *Italianità* into Stravinsky's *recherche du temps perdu*, or into Teutonic *Neue Sachlichkeit* and Viennese twelve-tone expressionism.

Roman Goffredo Petrassi and Istrian Luigi Dallapiccola are curiously complementary characters. Dallapiccola soon learnt to feel, with tragic intensity, that music is moving fast toward some *ultima Thule* of atomized harmonies and disintegrating structures. Petrassi, though aware of such distorting and disrupting forces, would go on acting upon the belief that music, come what may, has its indestructibly perennial side.

A decade before Boulez, Dallapiccola has been the first Latin musician to adhere to the Viennese grammar and syntax without having ever been – like Roberto Gerhard – a Schoenberg pupil. And he seems thereby to have followed Nietzsche's and Gide's advice, and to have looked for an influence as remote as possible from his own natural inborn leanings. The young Dallapiccola was nothing less than a latter-day romantic in quest of music's quintessential and abstract aspects. His ear and his instincts were then, and still are, an Italian realist's, with a strong sense of music's here-and-now as represented by simple, static, near-folksong or near-Gregorian monody, by the square rhythms of hymn-tune and march-tune, by the substantial and homely sound of bells, and by

116

Pan's flute (or even Marsyas's, in whose honour he wrote, as late as 1942, a racy ballet score), rather than by Apollo's idealistic lyre. Such is the stuff Dallapiccola's early works are made of: for example, *Sei cori di Michel Angelo il Giovane* and *Inni* for three pianos – excellent works, by no means obscured by those to follow. And at every step of his career he reverts now and then – with settings of Goethe and Greek poets, a *Sonata canonica* for piano, after Paganini, and *Tartiniana* – to 'music considered as an entertainment', to music written by the Busoni-ist that Dallapiccola, even twelve-tone Dallapiccola, has never ceased to be.

In 1935 at the Prague ISCM Festival he heard Schoenberg's *Variations* for orchestra, Berg's *Lulu* Suite and Webern's Concerto, Op. 24, and – a composer in search of method and mastery – became a convert to uprooted tonality and ever unquiet and effervescently chromatic design. But in his instinctive reactions he remained the old securely rooted realist of cool musical sound and colour. The ensuing debate between composer's decisions and musician's nature developed another (and again very Italian) side of Dallapiccola: his talent for the dramatic. A talent not so much for writing opera as for turning any score into a battle or at least a *Kriegspiel* of conflicting musical impulses. Take his *Canti di Prigionia* for voices and chamber orchestra: nothing could be more pointedly made up of contrasts. The modal (and Berliozian) *Dies Irae* motive incessantly joins with twelve-tone rows; dark-coloured melody attuned to the messages of doomed prisoners – Mary, Queen of Scots, Boëthius and Savonarola – but framed in most unromantic *teintes-froides* scoring, rhythms of very un-Viennese tranquil regularity prominent in music whose expression of claustrophobic *morbidezza* stems from *Wozzeck*. So many contradictory impulses, are dramatically and convincingly welded into this first of Dallapiccola's works in the new manner (1938–41).

Dallapiccola's style denotes an unforeseen reversal of the romantic situation. To express their rebellious mood and convictions Romantics were looking for a rebellious musical vocabulary. Their modernity, down to anti-romantic Debussy's means – as Monteverde's had meant, or Haydn's – a breaking away from convention. With Dallapiccola – once more a harbinger of post-Second-World-War avantgarde – it is modernity's turn to become a convention: the conventional acceptance of music's 'dialectical moving-on' on the road of its history. Modernity is much less than before

117

requested to be pugnacious and protesting. It has itself moved on: from the *nolentem-trahunt* ' battle-of-*The-Rite-of-Spring*' stage to the *volentem-ducunt* ISCM, Donaueschingen and Royan Festival stage. Yet for a composer born in 1904 the modern idiom still bore the imprint of its rebellious origins, and Dallapiccola, a romantic turned inside out, was looking for dramatic subject-matter to suit his chosen vocabulary.

In *Canti di Liberazione* (1955) the idea of *Dominus quasi vir pugnator* is evoked, and Pharaoh and his warriors going down 'like stones' in the 'abyss of the Red Sea'; with *Rencesvals* (1946), the harshest episode of *La Chanson de Roland* is provided with a piano accompaniment of apposite dourness; *Requiescant* (1958), half spiritual, half secular, is a cantata about cruel bereavement; in *Preghieri* (1962) on poems by his 'brother in spirit' Murillo Méndes, we find *Thou who art the true son of God, unnail humanity from its Cross*; and in *Parole di San Paolo* (1964): *Though I speak with the tongues of men and of angels and have no charity, I am become as sounding brass or tinkling cymbal* – and, quoted by Dallapiccola, this famous text may well remind us that none but tragically minded musicians should have access to the vocabulary of *Erwartung* and of Webern's chamber music.

Dallapiccola could not but be tempted by *drama per musica*; and his first, pre-twelve-tone opera *Volo di Notte* (1939), could not but achieve success, being a competent piece of operatic realism (if not *verismo*) adroitly varied and well balanced, though with something of a hollow ring about its score as well as its story – an epic in praise of a pseudo-Nietzschean pioneer of commercial aviation who qualifies as a superman by letting his subordinates take deadly risks.

Il Prigioniero (1948) displays the true Dallapiccola transfer of realistic substance into the insubstantial domain of dream or nightmare. In sixteenth-century Flanders a prisoner of the Holy Office is subjected to 'Torture by Hope': his liberation, his gaoler tells him, seems imminent, thanks to the success of the Flemish uprising. The door of his cell chances to be unlocked, and by still greater chance two monks, met in the precincts of the gaol, fail to notice the fugitive. Starry night, fragrant spring and freedom are within reach. '*Fratello*, why do you seek to leave me, at the blessed moment of your being rid of mortal life and guilt?' asks the Inquisitor, appearing from nowhere.

In 1941 Dallapiccola edited Monteverde's *Il Ritorno d' Ulisse in patria*. In 1969 he completed his own *Ulysses*, the most accomplished of his operas and perhaps musically too uncompromising a score to be a fully effective opera. As Nausicaa's charmer, as the haunted, metaphysical adventurer visiting Hades, as the pitiless liquidator of the suitors, Dallapiccola's Ulysses may well be – among all those set to music – the most truly Homeric one. And, to take a classical hero and express him, as such, in the least classical of harmonies and colours was an enterprise for which Dallapiccola was well equipped. But writing his own libretto he added another bold contrast. This Ulysses never agrees to return to Ithaca. Since Troy he seems to have travelled, not for twenty years, but for twenty centuries. No longer Hellenic and Homeric he refuses to be committed to anything but restlessness, and returns alone to the sea – a dissonant and unresolved Flying Dutchman who will not take Penelope for a Senta.

Nevertheless no dramatic text is needed to make Dallapiccola compose dramatically. Whether it be orchestral music like his *Variations* (1954) or chamber music like *Due studi* for violin and piano (1947), or *Ciacona, Intermezzo ed Adagio* for solo cello (1945), it is always, however ingeniously varied, the same vitality of sound enclosed in ascetic musical architecture. *Piccola musica notturna* (1954) is a Mozartian title, but it is not intended to be, as one might imagine, a promise of lightheartedness. Read Machado's lines quoted on the title page:

> It is a lovely summer night. . . .
> High in the sky the moon, and on the tower
> the illuminated dial of the clock.
> I walk in this old village
> alone, like a phantom.

A remarkably apt quotation indeed: an atmospheric comment on one particular score of Dallapiccola's and a fairly accurate description of all his scores' fabric – metallic, luminous solidity its warp, ghostlike fugacity its woof.

The case of Goffredo Pertassi (born 1904) is simpler, yet his is a rare case among modern musicians: both open-minded and single-minded. A 'pure' musician who, takes music to be *l'art pour l'art*. But this creed, more often an aesthete's, is for Petrassi a craftsman's. He wrote one of his best scores (and no doubt his best

I

known) *Coro di Morti* on deeply disillusioned, almost despairing, words of Leopardi – and he set them to music in June, 1940, when, as he tells us, 'nothing could have come nearer to [my] mood than the mood of these words'. One can easily imagine the tormented music Dallapiccola would have torn out of them. Petrassi calls his piece a 'dramatic madrigal': his music is meant neither to depict anxiety nor to translate Leopardi into music: it is meant to provide Leopardi's poetry with *musica seriosa*, with an unruffled, madrigalesque setting.

This taste for objectivity and distaste for any sort of emotional over-emphasis had ceased, long before 1940, to imply militant antiromanticism (see page 25). Like Hindemith, whose influence can be traced in his early scores (e.g. *Introduzione ed Allegro* for violin and eleven instruments, 1933) Petrassi is, rather than an antiromantic composer, a neo-classically-minded a-romantic one. And for Italian Petrassi it has been more justifiable than for any contemporary German musician to indulge in neo-classical leanings. Hindemith could not help stemming from late-romantic Brahms and post-romantic Reger, and his back-to-Bach was hardly workable. Musical craftsmen in the 1925 manner have always been ill at ease when referring back to a metaphysical craftsman like Bach; and in fact Hindemith's chose his sponsors among ill-defined sets of anonymous half-mediaeval, half-imaginary *Meistermusikanten* and *Stadtpfeifers*. In contrast Petrassi (as for Casella and Malipiero immediately before him) there were grand old madrigalists by the dozen, Venetians and others, every one of them expressive without ceasing to be decoratively objective, and all of them legitimate intercessors for Italian composers of the twentieth century *renascimento*.

Petrassi allows them to lead him a good deal of the way, but not the whole way. He appears to be, perhaps reluctantly, aware of the perils – first of all the risk of spuriousness – that threaten neoclassicisms and revivals. He is, after all, too modern not to have some doubts about music's being perennial. And, to de-dogmatize his style and rid it of archaism, he resorts to dazzling technique, versatility and virtuosity. His one-act opera *Il Cordovano* (1948), a classic comedy on the old 'cuckold miser and charming young adulteress' theme, is so brilliantly rigged out with every tricky gadget of sophisticated harmony and counterpoint and – in a style that calls for *commedia dell' arte* – leaves so little room for *com-*

media dell' arte improvisation, that perfect performance is likely to be as infrequent as it would be impressive.

Or again with *Nonsense* for *a cappella* choir (1952) Petrassi enjoys letting 'art for art's sake' make fun of itself, takes the 'surrealist adventures' of Edward Lear's characters for his text, and introduces flute-playing old man and long-chinned spinster as exponents of craftsmanship that triumphs over everything from harpstrings and canonic pedantries to 'sarpints' and polytonal side-slips.

Written in 1951, the cantata *Noche Oscura* (words by St John of the Cross) prolongs the style of *Coro di Morti* – grandeur and restraint blended – and may well be his most important work. But none is more significant than his less *serioso* and less straight-forward string quartet (1956–7). Here the complete craftsman seems strangely bent on escaping from the logic and consistency that complete craftsmanship stands for. The musical discourse is deliberately erratic and pervaded by a keen, impish, and purely musical sort of irony which, regardless of the expressive content of this quartet, marks its construction, its way of moving about, again and again giving preference to the discontinuous, the unforeseen, and even the incongruous. Yet, the *Quartetto* ends with an inversely unforeseen return to calm and commonsense, which in this context sounds unreal and touching – not unlike the final awakening of Don Quixote.

The craftsman, grown sceptic and no longer convinced of crafts-manship's self-sufficiency, remembers Debussy and lets his *Séré-nade* be *interrompue*, just as he arrives at the brink of joining Boulez's *artisanat furieux*. With seemingly conservative Petrassi, no less than with advanced Dallapiccola, we are on the doorstep of avantgarde.

Dallapiccola

11 Avantgarde:
Ciphers, games and spells

No one is ever at the head of Time's procession. The past catches at his coat tails sometimes, and sometimes jostles and shoves him on and sometimes the future drags him forward with unseen hands and sometimes, when he's least expecting it, pushes him back – as we push back a kitten that's over-eager for a dish of milk ...
Charles Morgan's Judge

Post-Second-World-War modernism was, to begin with, a desperate and partially successful attempt on the part of 'contemporary music' to recover its old classical and romantic prerogative. Whatever Chopin's or Beethoven's or Bach's or Monteverde's popularity and importance – the avantgarde, in France and elsewhere, proclaimed that Copernicus was wrong (see page 21): that in the twentieth century, twentieth-century music should have its place, not on the fringe of the musical carpet, but at its centre, as its main pattern; and that contemporary music should prove its contemporariness by sounding unlike any music written and heard before. No nostalgic side glances at the eighteenth century, at renaissance madrigals, at mediaeval modes or at Egyptian shepherds' flute: no donnish toying with out-of-the-way allusions and quotations. During the twenties, when pastiche and revivals were part of the up-to-date musicians' stock in trade, Constant Lambert remarked that 'today every composer's overcoat has its corresponding hook in the cloak-room of the past': an attitude most unlike Wagner's, for instance, who, if told 'that you admired his operas because they were "like" Cimarosa ... would probably have kicked you out of the house'.

In the early fifties any avantgarde musician would have reacted

122

most emphatically in the manner of Constant's Wagner. Read Boulez commenting on his *Structures* for two pianos (1952):

My purpose has been based on the following idea: my vocabulary should be cleansed of every trace of traditional ways of treating pattern, phrase, development or form. I would aim at and, element after element, look for an entirely new and self-sufficient synthesis, unadulterated by extraneous substances (such as reminiscences of former styles). I have no taste for borrowing my manner of using intervals from one source, my way with rhythm from a second, my 'idea of form' from a third. . . .

For the composer this means never to be caught napping in his control of a most intricate and exclusive technique, devised to bar ninety-nine 'vocables' before admitting the hundredth. For the listener it means to be presented with music without the shadow of a motive apt to be memorized by an ear in search of something to be hummed or whistled; without the shadow of a rhythm to march or dance to; without any landmarks of symmetry to cling to. And negative though this description looks, there is a singular vital strength about these anti-derivative whiffs of music and extracts of sound, which so gleefully incur the backward music critic's favourite cliché of 'clever and quite interesting maybe, but NO MUSIC'. During a quarter of a century this supposed anti-music has never ceased to appeal to large audiences that do not mainly consist of hippies and other angry young people, of snobs welcoming the latest chic or morbid dilettanti in quest of musical satanism. Like it or not, musical modernity is popular today, and popular for modernity's sake. And this unprecedented popularity has led audiences to unprecedented ways of reacting: at almost every concert given by the Domaine Musical (a group founded in Paris by Boulez) hisses and catcalls greet, not an exaggeratedly 'advanced' item, but the item dismissed – rightly or mistakenly – as conventional, as too 'normal-sounding'.

Yet, however radically intent upon innovation, a musical technique cannot be conjured up out of the void: it has to refer to some pre-existent method. Thus it is not surprising that Pierre Boulez (born 1924) should, to begin with, have used the Viennese twelve-tone technique – that technique of permanent protest and suspense which takes every note of the chromatic scale to be a leading note and a dominant and then prevents that note from leading anywhere and from dominating over any definite tonality. Before the war this technique had scarcely been heard of in France, but about 1945 young French students of composition were initiated in Schoenberg's system by a very conscientious and devoted professor, René Leibowitz. Boulez, then one of these students, took especially to Webern, who (like Schoenberg and Berg) considered the tonal cadence to be outworn, but moreover (and unlike Schoenberg and Berg) questioned the validity of any principle of construction derived from the tonal cadence. Before long, however, Boulez contrived to go beyond Webern's methods, and to turn away from Webern's aesthetics.

As to technique Boulez's innovation consisted of applying the serial principle not only – Schoenberg fashion – to (distorted and atonal) melody, harmony and polyphony but also to every other element of musical matter and form: timbre, metre, dynamics (from *ppp* to *fff*) and attack (from *staccatissimo* to *legatissimo*). As with the twelve notes of the chromatic scale, all these elements were forthwith arranged in discontinuous 'rows' of patterns, the rule being that no pattern should re-appear before the whole series has unfolded, and that the entire piece should derive its 'structure' from one single formula – a formula that Boulez, with a mathematician's pedantic glee, called the 'parameter' chosen to underlie all the patterns' shape and succession. Paradoxically and no doubt fortunately, this mathematical method – so abstract in theory, appearance and definition, has an adventurously practical *raison d'être*. Like Marvell's Love 'It is begotten by despair upon impossibility', for it is a mechanism devised to escape from the detested staleness of inescapable tradition; to exclude the obvious and pre-ordain the unforeseen; to exclude even the remotest reminiscence of, say, Rossini's delightful and irritating 'cadences-and-no-end'; and to provide us, at any moment in the course of musical events, with the expectation of the unexpected.

Such already had been Webern's methods and intentions, in his enigmatic aphorisms-in-sound, but Webern's allusive approach had been that of a disillusioned mandarin. His *mis*leading notes are always soft-spoken and mostly *pp*, and every single one of them fraught with nostalgia. His message is the swan-song of the symphonic hero who has learnt to think that the subtlest music is distilled from lost battles. Not so Boulez, whose emblem would be, not the dying valedictory swan but the lively cockerel saluting a new dawn. He might admit – he is by no means naïve – that his method is begotten upon impossibility, but not by despair. Rather by aggressive vitality, and a boyish and Beethovenish, 'I'll teach you and reach you, if not through the door, then through the wall.'

The influence of Boulez's doctrine and of the practice he laid down in vocal and orchestral scores like *Le Soleil des eaux* and *Visage nuptial*, and in piano music like his first two Sonatas (1946–8) and his *Structures*, for two pianos, has been immediate, widespread and lasting. Everywhere, from New Zealand to Toronto by way of Darmstadt and Madrid, young musicians entered the scene with music made of hints and anacoluthons, of splinters and sparks, of intervals jumping over several octaves, piccolos at the top of their voices answering double-bass' whispers, of sudden outbursts and sudden silence, of lopsided or truncated metre, of sprays of demisemiquavers and the long-resonance of gongs – in short of every form of suddenness and abruptness that might have been specially devised to nonplus the ear and infuriate the philistine. And, strange to witness, by 1950, at the very moment when the obligation to ignore all precedents seemed to have marooned any new composer on the cliff of his private imagination and ingenuity, nine new composers out of ten were, on the contrary, ready to avail themselves of a newly evolved cosmopolitan *lingua franca*. This was strange but not inexplicable: the Boulez of the fifties was nothing less than an exclusive aristocratic artist. Whether speaking, writing or playing he deported himself as a craftsman. Not, of course, like Hindemith or Petrassi, a member of the musicians' guild, but a member of that *artisanat furieux* met with in one of his texts (by René Char) who 'imagines Peru's treasures on the edge of his knife'. His method of making music that seems out of joint (but is in fact throughout constructed and controlled) gave a novel fascination to the act of composing – a fascination that springs from its difficulty and complexity. 'I worked at it like an insect' he once said to me about a score unfortunately and irretrievably lost in a Cologne hotel – and enables late twentieth century composers to forget, at least for a while, everything else concerning music's past and present, and rejoice in an encouraging *construo, ergo sum*. The listener, too, caught up in the structural labyrinth, is fascinated and, according to temperament, either lets himself be devoured by the Minotaur without asking questions or else, thanks to Ariadne, enjoys the adventure without losing his head.

But as a *lingua franca* this 'structural method' – that war machine devised to kill convention – would soon itself become a convention: the unexpected it had to produce became dangerously expected, even monotonous. A second method had to be devised and to win the avantgarde's favour: the complementary method of 'open forms'.

Another *cliché* dear to anti-modernists would ironically come true: 'Nobody would notice if, instead of the composer's, other notes were played'. For 'open forms' mean that the score is no longer wholly written out but, at least partially, merely outlined. Within the limits of certain schemes mapped out with graphic symbols – curves, dots, arrows, and other hieroglyphics, which often combine into pleasant visual rhythms – the performers improvise on their own initiative or guided by a conductor who signals when, where and how to start or to stop. Nothing anarchical about this sort of incomplete notation, which has had its precedents: mediaeval *neumes*, seventeenth and eighteenth century figured basses. In every score ever written there are elements that are essential to the music's style and meaning, and others that are not. An old textbook of orchestration shows a surprising amount of different and equally workable dispositions of the same conclusive triad. In Bach's and Rameau's accompaniments identical chords can be differently spaced. And in a passage written in 1970 a certain quality and colour of massive, or strident, or bleak, or screeching, or garrulous or mumbling sound may be the essence of the music aimed at, and may be obtained with identical effect from combining notes and sequences of notes, and altering their order, in dozens of ways.

Boulez, in his college days, was so proficient in mathematics that his father, himself a mathematician, strongly disapproved of his decision to enter the Conservatoire. And mathematical thought and practice again are another leading avantgarde composer's forte. But in contrast to Boulez, the man of musical discontinuity, Iannis Xenakis (born 1922), an architect and for years Le Corbusier's collaborator and often his deputy, has taken continuous continuity for his principle of composition. Nothing proves a better symbol and a clearer instance of continuity of sound, than a *glissando* (which annihilates all the discontinuities of diatonic, chromatic, natural or tempered scales). In *Metastasis* (1954), the score that first made his reputation, all the orchestra's strings start out from the same central G, and then by *glissandi* of different speeds for each player, the sound unfolds fanwise until it reaches an all-out chromatic twelve-tone chord. As mathematicians deal with *quanta*, Xenakis composes, not with notes but with *ensembles* of notes. He obtains, for example, music foreseeable in its shape, yet unforeseeable in its enunciation, by scattering the contents of a bag of intervals over his staves like a shower of raindrops splashing, rebounding and resounding on a tin roof: *viz* with total irregularity at first hearing, yet in retrospect with mathematically measurable regularity according to the rules of probability.

His piano concerto *Eonta* (1964) is so named in homage to the Ionian philosophy of 'Being' (as opposed to that Heraclitean 'Becoming' that presided – or at least could have presided – over centuries of Western music): a *pronunciamiento* in favour of 'music-as-sound' that *is* (as opposed to 'music-as-motive' that *develops*). Meantime, and quite unphilosophically, the scattering of notes over the keyboard offers all the toil and pleasure of super-Lisztian virtuosity to acrobatic player and dazzled listener. And, in guise of an orchestral accompaniment, ponderous and masterful brass is called in, ordered to play sometimes near the piano, sometimes in the background, and not entrusted with any design or motive, but used for its contrasting and varied sound value.

Variation and variegation of sound values is one of the main issues in avantgarde music. Even the composer of the eminently percussive *Rite of Spring* never dreamt of the prominence and diversity that was going to be given to percussion, indigenous or exotic: drums of every size (wooden, metallic or membranous), bells, rods, marimbas, tomtoms, tamtams and what not, to be whipped, hammered or grazed. Pierre Schaeffer's *musique concrète* provides composers with all sorts of sound material won by manipulation or distortion of natural noises and timbres. A rolling box is used to produce rapping tones and a trumpet for its clangorous notes. They are used concretely, i.e. regardless of traditional habits and connotations. To be 'concrete' a trumpet has to forget all about warlike or joyous fanfares.

This avantgarde approach to music, sound and noises had in fact been anticipated in Luigi Russolo's *Futurist Manifesto* (1913), which catalogued the 'six families of the futurist orchestra's noises' from 'booms and thunder claps' to 'wheezes and sobs'. But with electronics, with speeding up, slowing down, mixing and every sort of procrustean elongating and chopping of sound, Russolo's bold futurist programme has been outbidden by a long chalk. And the composer's imagination has to take the risk of drowning in the cataracts of tone-colours that flood the composer's palette.

Even without recourse to microphone and loudspeaker novel effects can be extracted from ready-to-hand sources. Xenakis uses his violins and cellos not merely as stringed instruments to be bowed or plucked, but also as precious boxes to be knocked with fingertips or knuckles. In *Nuits* (1968) for unaccompained voices vocal polyphony comprises lines sung, lines spoken, lines mumbled, lines laughed and lines spluttered.

Luciano Berio (born 1925) – remarkable since his student days and then successively as a composer in the style of Berg and a director of the electronic workshop in Milan – is by now one of the most original and independent composers. In his *Sequenze* (1963–66), written for different solo instruments, an oboe or a piano are by turns allowed or forbidden to sound 'like themselves'. We are reminded of a charming fairy tale: the king has pledged his word to marry a penniless and shrewd beauty if she contrives to proceed from her native hut to his palace 'neither clothed, nor naked, neither walking nor riding, nor skating, nor carried by man, woman or vehicle'. She triumphs by stripping, wrapping herself in a fishing net and hanging on to a horse's tail, her toes brushing the road. Faced with a similar predicament for having pitched his tent in musical no-man's land – no-previous-composer's land at any rate – the avantgarde musician resorts to inventing sequences of sound that are neither inside nor outside the realm of music : half composer's child, half computer's and tape-machine's offspring; neither clad in melodic and harmonic garments, nor naked noise; and vocally or instrumentally conveyed by voices or violins that sound like percussion, to run their course neither as non-committal improvisation, nor as definitely rounded-off compositions.

As produced by and addressed to twentieth-century ears, nerves, and minds, avantgarde music seems to have two roots and a double significance. Vastly enjoying its complexity of rules – never have programme notes and composers' declarations so copiously and complacently dwelt on explanations of technique – it is, first, a game to be played by composers and performers, often invited to decipher and prolong composers' ciphers, and to be watched by perfunctorily initiated listeners. Xenakis (among others) has even imagined and charted competitive games – *Stratégie* (1962) – to be fought out by two conductors heading two orchestral teams. (And this explains why, in spite of so many variations in sound-value, avantgarde compositions are so often monochrome in expression: chess and patience, too, are ever varied, yet always of the same character.)

André Boucourechliev, a French composer of Bulgarian extraction (born 1925), calls a set of works (for string quartet, chamber ensemble or solo piano *Archipelagos* (1967–70), and explains – quite poetically – that by following the chart of his open forms the performing navigators will on each performance 'discover new channels between the islands and unexpected capes and recesses'. Yet successive and very different readings of *Archipelagos* (as they have been recorded) are apt illustrations of *plus ça change, plus c'est la même chose*. And no wonder: musical compositions used to be somehow like letters by which composers corresponded with listeners. Avantgarde composers seem to be habitually averse to composing and sending-off such letters. They are content with sending specimens of their handwriting. Quite often a very original handwriting, and even a fascinating one – as Boucourechliev's certainly is. Yet hardly capable of meaning more than can be taken in, once and for ever, at the first glance.

Apart from being a game, a manifestation of *homo ludens* (as the Dutch philosopher Huizinga has called him), avantgarde music appears secondly to be a manifestation of *homo turbatus* – of disturbed mortals. It is distilled from sound flavoured with noise, and – to allure the innocent – with a grain extracted from the shadow of music by composers who are dispensers of musical magic or (more prosaically) dispensers of musical drugs. Thus the old half-forgotten magical connotations of percussion, the fascination of Boucourechliev's or Spanish Luís de Pablo's (born 1939) sound-graphs, the rites and rules of the game, and the protracted and hypnotic sonorous monochrome come into their full significance. The necessity of keeping the operation severely under (mathematical or other) control proves its seriousness – and the risks implied. For listen! Again and again it sounds as if it were ominously on the brink of escaping control, of unchaining music's Caliban and wringing musical Ariel's neck.

Western music, however, and modern music in particular, is too adventurous, mobile and restless to dwell for more than a short while in the narrowness of magic circles (whatever their prestige), to make a habit of drugs (whatever their potency), or to stick to the principle of avantgarde music's self-sufficiency (however flattering to the composer's pride). Before long it appears that Copernicus has not accepted defeat, and new items enter the avantgarde scene, which are no less avantgarde than the others for having come to terms with the past.

Among the attempts at resuming contact and dialogue, Sylvano Bussotti's (born 1931) Teatro Strumentale – *La Passion selon Sade* (1966) is no doubt the most eccentric. *Commedia dell' arte* is evoked, Italian opera made fun of, *bel canto* quoted – not without parody. The orchestra is placed on the stage : *sinfonia* is essential – and why shouldn't *dramma per musica* lead up to *opera per orchestra?* The conductor directs with one hand, the other being about the prima donna's waist. Another love scene consists in the solo cellist's dreamy caressing of his cello's voluptuous rotundities. Well, isn't *amore* the main subject of operatic *sinfonia?*

Less eccentric but just as baroque, Berio, in one movement of *his* symphony (*Sinfonia*, 1968) embeds a whole unabridged Mahler Scherzo in a polyphony of shouts and other avantgarde sound-values. Venetian (and Schoenbergian) Luigi Nono (born 1924) decided, years ago, that his music should be both avantgarde and resolutely anti-highbrow – a decision rooted in his strong political convictions. This led him to combine, in works like *Hiroshima* (1962) or *La Fabbrica illuminata* (1965), an aristocratically distinguished technique with a style that derives its undeniably popular appeal from the aesthetics of the film (but not from the aesthetics of film music). Of late, however, his *Contrappunto dialettico alla Mente* (1968) – no less politically engaged a score and made of sound-material derived from Venetian market-cries – is also intended to be a homage to Bianchieri, and old Venetian and in no way plebeian Madrigalist. In Nicolo Castiglioni's delightful radio-opera (1961), after Lewis Carroll's *Through the Looking-Glass,* electronically manipulated voices do not blush for neighbouring with a Monteverdean pastiche. And, Xenakis admits melodic motives and Greek modes to his music for the *Oresteia* (1966).

Boulez himself has long ceased to be the ultra of avantgardist insularity we knew in 1950. After his sonatas – written to end The Sonata, as James Joyce wrote novels to end The Novel – *Le Marteau sans maître* (1954) owed the greater part of its exceptional success to reminding us of both *Pierrot Lunaire* (conceived by a Schoenberg who, according to Nicolas Nabokov, knew about Japanese *No*) and of early Debussy's exoticism. *Le Marteau*'s xylophone indeed seems to refer more than once to the gamelan's *Gambang Kayu*. And in his subsequent scores – *Pli selon pli* (1967), *Éclats* (1966), *Cummings is the Poet*, it is *late* Debussy that is unmistakably present. Not the archaising, byzantine or baroque Debussy of *Le Martyre* or *En blanc et noir*, but the Debussy of *Jeux* and of the *Études* for piano with their rarified and thinned-out subject matter and the utter precision and economy of their diction. Every trace of Boulez's former boisterous aggressiveness has been discarded. Magic and other demagogic effects are disclaimed. The blend of instrumental and vocal timbres scintillates in ever shifting and ever luminous shades, never in glaring colours. Not only late Debussy, but all that has ever been 'late' in Western music, late Beethoven in particular, seems to be revisited and subjected to spectral analysis in both the adjective's senses. The magic that subsists is the magic of a very strange ascetic hedonism, and – again as with Debussy – of remoteness, of a merciless rejection of the obvious and the facile – especially of the facile *clichés* of the difficult.

The 'furious craftsman' has been turned into an aristocrat *malgré lui.*

Boulez

Postlude:
A batch of independents

It is not always timidity that, by 1970, keeps a musician outside the avantgarde movement. Avantgarde, as we have seen, has its *lingua franca*, its code, its symbols and its attitude – so surprisingly un-questioned by any avantgardist. In consequence it needs no less courage to reject chartered (and well established) anti-conventions than to reject chartered (and ramshackle) conventions. And to keep clear of conformity to either conformism or anti-conformism a contemporary composer has to show uncommon audacity and even quite often, a disposition not unlike Red Indian's cunning.

Such a composer at once incurs the reproach of putting the clock back, of trying in vain to stem the current of history of music – in short, of writing superfluous music. A heinous reproach, and 'parti-sans of progress', by resorting to it when met with musicians they think less progressive than themselves, merely prove that they are trying to ignore a heinous fact, *viz*, that contemporary music, whether avantgarde or not, fails (according to that invidious fellow Copernicus) to count as a household necessity for nine professional musicians out of ten, and for ninety-nine concert-goers in a hundred. The crux is that many composers, some very succesful, have indeed written and are every day writing unnecessary music. In this respect the twentieth century differs little from the nineteenth: try listening to some of the scores whose merits are extolled in Schumann's writings. But in the century that produced in the same year *Oedipus Rex* and Berg's *Kammerkonzert* it stands to reason that this question of musical value and validity cannot be a question of camp and tendency. Any composer may be a musical Cavalier, or a musical Roundhead. The question is whether a given musical machine, devised to honour the king or to honour the Covenant, proves to be motioned by a battery of high or of low voltage.

Henri Sauguet and Vittorio Rieti are unequivocally Cavaliers. Neo-classicists, unwilling to consider modern music and musical modernity as problematic affairs, they came of age with and have ever remained faithful to Les Six, and decided to pitch their tents in *one* province of Stravinsky's realm – the sheltered province where *Pulcinella, Apollo, Dumbarton Oaks* and *Le Baiser de la fée* are situated.

Henri Sauguet (born 1901) has much in common with Auric. His reputation like Auric's rests upon his competent ballet scores: *La Chatte* (1927) *Les Mirages* (1943), *Les Forains* (1945), *La Dame aux camélias* (1957). He is certainly an unequal composer who seems to think – at least that's the way his music sounds – that excess of self-criticism would mean lack of sincerity. But his intelligence, wit, and his catlover's kind-heartedness, which corrects his silky man-of-the-worldliness, are reflected in his works and are responsible for many endearing and some moving pages. *One* opus of Sauguet's is without parallel: a masterly short unaccompanied monody, written for the farewell concert of his friend Doda Conrad.

With Vittorio Rieti (born 1898) intelligence never ceases to keep fantasy and fancy under control. Les Six – save Honegger – accepted a good deal of amateurishness as part of their predilection for the unpedantic and the straightforward. Rieti likes, and imagines, the same sort of music as Poulenc, but writes this music with a thoroughly unamateurish precision and certitude of purpose – and with a sense of proportion, economy and purity of style that Poulenc never cared for. Poulenc's music is pastiche and reminiscence all over: Rieti's neo-classicism – clear-cut, faultlessly scored and of perfectly lucid construction – contrives to summon up an eighteenth century spirit without recourse to eighteenth century matter.

Whether ballet or opera (*Le Bal*, 1929; Don Perlimplin), symphony (for example his Fourth, 1942), incidental music (Molière's *L'École des femmes*), or chamber music, or concerto for harpsichord, there is always something pleasant and tasty, and something exemplary about Rieti's scores: they are, all of them, achieved by a brilliant professor of non-professorial composition.

Henri Barraud belongs to the generation of Les Six, and Henri

Dutilleux has, as a professor of Composition at the Paris Conservatoire, succeeded Milhaud and Jolivet (Jeune France). But, much more in pursuit of musical construction than Les Six – again, and as usual, Honegger excepted – and much less addicted to 'espressivo at any cost' (as Nietzsche would say) than Jeune France, they both stem from Roussel: they are both born symphonists and polyphonists.

If we take Barraud's music from the technical angle – and his jealously 'pure' musicianship calls for this sort of approach – we soon find out that his originality resides in his being a symphonist and also a modalist: a double allegiance that immediately seems to head for difficulty and paradox, for symphony means tension and development, and modes – especially Barraud's Gregorian modes – are static and tranquil, unwilling to get on the move. Barraud, however, has derived his style from this *prima-facie* incompatibility. His music is not romantically dramatic; there is something quietly epic about his long-drawn modal unisons as they appear, their gravity underlined by iambic rhythm, in almost every one of his scores, from his early Preludes for strings (1928–34) up to his recent *Études* for orchestra.

Modern modal writing too often escapes into some golden age of musical ease and of innocence attested by the absence of 'wrong notes'. Barraud, whose modal lines, as soon as they cease being monody, make for an unmitigated dissonance of conflicting counterpoint, wants his Gregorianism to be militant: its archaic, mediaeval connotations evoke Albi Cathedral, both a sanctuary and a fortress: stones bristling with metaphysics and determination.

Le Testament Villon (1945) – a perilous enterprise after Debussy's Villon settings – is successfully carried out by linking *a cappella* madrigals with recitatives for solo voice accompanied by harpsichord. *Le Mystère des Saints Innocents* (1946) is one of the best examples, since Caplet, of French spiritual music, text by Charles Péguy (1873-1914), who, as a poet, was a pugnacious archaizer not unlike Barraud. His Piano Concerto (1939) is effective, distinguished and its style as though met with at the crossroads of Roussel's and Stravinsky's. Three operatic scores are *La Farce de Maître Pathelin*, *Numance* and *Lavinia*. The first, based on the mediaeval farce, is the most congenial to Barraud's talent, *Numance* (text by Salvador de Madariaga after Cervantes) being over-ambitious as a tragedy and *Lavinia* too unambitious a comedy.

Somewhat surprisingly Barraud the symphonist is at his best, not in his symphonies (1956–7), but in *La Symphonie de Numance* (1952) which, extracted from *Numance,* makes better musical tragedy with none but symphonic means, and in his two *Rapsodies.* The *Rapsodie Cartésienne* (1960) epitomizes, in its content as in its name, the plight of modern music – and of a good deal of other music: to be both all nerves and all brains; rhapsodic *and* Cartesian; improvisatory and even fantastic; and nevertheless thought-out, responsible, and controlled. In the *Rapsodie Dionysienne* (1962), as in the subsequent *Études* for orchestra, Barraud, especially in his dealings with percussion, goes a good way towards meeting the avantgarde.

With Henri Dutilleux (born 1916) listeners of very different musical creeds, predilections and prejudices feel safe. His symphonic architecture is powerful without ever being oppressive or pompous. His polyphony is of the French and modern sort, as invented by Berlioz and re-invented by Debussy: apt to superpose elements that differ in expression, rhythm, metre and tempo. Moreover his dissonant harmony and skilfully distorted melody sounds unusual enough not to be censured by the avantgarde-minded. Yet, on the other hand, without reminding us of any well established score in particular, almost any page of Dutilleux's reminds us of well established music in general. For all its harmonic dissonance and melodic distortion the sound and pattern of this music can be traced back to familiar sound and pattern. An ever-romanticizing conductor like Charles Münch, quite helpless when confronted with any score of Stravinsky's written after 1950, felt quite at ease with Dutilleux's Second Symphony (1959) and his *Métaboles* (1964).

Dutilleux's technique is astounding. No contemporary composer knows better how to plan a score and how to round it off, how to give his piano, his fiddles, his woodwind, his brass their exact due, and – as Cocteau would say – 'how far one should go when going too far' in modernism.

Classically numbered and neatly filled up to Op. 104 or thereabouts, Henri Martelli's works comprise music of every description: sacred and secular, vocal and instrumental, chamber music and symphonic music – faultlessly written and in faultless good taste.

135

And in every single one of his scores we find Martelli's unmistakably personal imprint: a *serioso* manner and a *scherzando* manner of his own. Two of his scores, however – one early and the other recent – go considerably further than this *maître mineur* elegance. *Bas-Reliefs assyriens* for orchestra was inspired by the monumental carvings on show in the British Museum. A concise yet imposing symphonic fresco: juxtaposed chords, instrumental colours and melodic contours chosen and blended to symbolize the granite white and grey (1928). *La Chanson de Roland* (revised 1964), after the old epic, is a full-size opera-oratorio, and though written in a very different style – Charlemagne has little in common with Assurbanipal – it is a similar study in musical liveliness and hieratic reticence. It has a very distinctive harmonic syntax, its tonality as it were circumscribed and occasionally dislodged by attacks from right and left – from the side of all-out dissonance and from the side of modalism. The style is of a mystery play, and the score one that Vaughan Williams might well have approved of, and one which should tempt unprejudiced conductors and imaginative opera directors, just as it should please singers for Martelli's superior handling of *recitativo drammatico*.

Martelli, born in Corsica (1895) and presiding over both the old Société Nationale and the French section of the less old (though no longer young) ISCM, is well known – at least in the 'inner circle'. Marcelle de Manziarly – half French, half Russian – most of the time seems unwilling to leave her ivory workshop. Among her contemporaries I know of no other case of so flagrant a discrepancy between a composer's achievement and that composer's presence – or rather absence – on the musical scene.

A pupil of Nadia Boulanger's, she appears to be the one true disciple of Stravinsky in France. Ever since the twenties and not by mimicry, but by natural affinity – she has followed Stravinsky's path, and proceeded from neo-classicism – that particular Stravinskian brand which varies rather than imitates the motives of classicism – to assimilating and, again, varying the motives of avantgarde. It is perhaps part of her Stravinsky-ism that she has treated her scores as so many problems to solve and so many pleasures to indulge in. Hence the rare and extremely enjoyable singleness of mind – of composer's mind – displayed in her works. Whatever her purpose – to adapt the patterns of a given form (for example a *passcaglia*) to the requirements of a given ensemble (a trio for flute, cello and piano), to balance solo piano, orchestral accompaniment and the 'spirit of percussion'; to evoke, from the point of view of a twentieth century musician, the attitude of the masters of the Notre Dame School at the dawn of polyphony and to put on the pure intellectual's mask when shaping a piano piece in accordance with the numerical arcana of a *magic square (Stances)*: in every instance we feel that she has accepted none but the most ingenious (and seemingly simplest) solution of her problem, effaced every trace of toil and made musical events run their course with playful relentlessness without looking right or left. Such are the unforgivably neglected scores twentieth-century music owes to Marcelle de Manziarly's talent, technique and wit, and to her rare sense of the musical and the human values that make the composition of scores worthwhile.

Let us wind up with the two independents that stand nearest to avantgarde. Fifty years ago Willem Pijper, the best Dutch composer of his day, reproached his countrymen with being over-interested in the ethical side of music: 'Going to concerts should be different from going to church, and writing scores different from writing homilies. But *you* comment on Bach's or Beethoven's "message" as if it were the Bible. Real musicians, and real music-lovers turn to music because singing, piping or drumming is pleasurable, and because they are entranced by the beauty of sound – or, maybe, even by the ugliness of sound.'

Pijper would have liked Claude Ballif (born 1924), whose approach to music and to composition is pleasantly free from the fear of taboos and the adoration of totems. In consequence he chooses his musical material with a winning and unusual naïvety. Such material may, or may not, be eccentric, scrappy or smooth, related or unrelated to melody or rhythm as practised yesterday or centuries ago.

To make such a baroque variety of elements combine in a piece of music that carries conviction he trusts his musician's common-sense, his sense of humour and his excellent technique, gained (after his passage at the Paris Conservatoire), in Berlin under Boris Blacher's tuition. Ballif's music is indeed singularly compelling: his 'pure music' – string quartets, string trios, duo sonatas, or his *Études* for seven instruments on diverse intervals – as well as his fantasies, named, in the manner of Satie, *Condensed Airs* or *Spare Parts* for piano (1953), *Hunting Cries* (1962) or *This and That* (1965) for orchestra. Or his *Études sur le souffle* – searching and haunting studies in madrigalesque and other musical values extracted from the enunciation of vowels.

In quite different style but no less bold, are his *Antiennes à la Vierge*: archaic vocal lines, an orchestral accompaniment of un-quiet and ill defined harmony – dissonant light, as it were, filtering through the ill defined colours of a stained-glass window.

Of Spanish origin, British by passport, Anglo-French by up-bringing and a Parisian by residence, Maurice Ohana (born 1914) is a legitimate descendant of De Falla. Guitar-minded and *cante jondo*-minded, and not without a certain harshness and a hidalgo's haughtiness of diction. And a tendency not so much to bridge as to efface the distance between archaism and the here-and-now, and between the sacred and the secular accents of music. If, in Boulez's view, the making of music is the affair of furious craftsmen, Ohana would rather apply to ecstatic minstrels. A work of such striking grandeur as *Cantigas* (1954) – with its allusions to Alfonso the Wise's original sacred monodies (thirteenth century) and to Debussy, and to Stravinsky's Debussy-inspired *Symphonies d'instruments à vent* – has been the result of this musical creed and practice.

With another hardly less impressive but very different score, *Cris*, for *a cappella* choir (1968) Ohana enlists under the avantgarde banner – not without demonstrating, *en passant*, that avantgardist experiments in combining singing, speaking and shouting vocal utterance can be traced back to flamenco style. Yet Ohana himself is quite ready to let himself be tempted into experimenting. If he did not invent the third-tone cithara, he is probably the first to have made it serviceable in a written score. And *Syllabaire pour Phèdre* (*Primer for Phaedra*, 1967), perhaps his best work to date, apart from resorting to electronics, is an experiment in opera through-out. Euripides's tragedy is reduced to essentials which can be fully expressed by musical symbols: anguish, wrath, passion, mortal conflict, pity. (A similar operatic condensation was aimed at, not long ago, in Blacher's *Abstrakte Oper*, but with a thorough-bass of parody quite alien to Phaedra). More than anything else, this *Phaedra* is a strange and admirable attempt to break through, as Debussy demanded, to the core of music, an attempt 'to uncover music's naked flesh'.

By way of De Falla back to Debussy with whom the adventure of nineteenth century music began. Indeed they are of the same family: the Egyptian shepherd playing his flute, the ecstatic minstrel, and the Hispano-Arabic muezzin delivering his invocatory chant.

Fifty years after Debussy's death, Ohana's works – near-avantgardist's music – read like a postscript, in the grand manner, to Debussy's. And this definition does not underrate Ohana's talent and stature – no more than it would mean underrating Rossini to define the best of his operas as glorious postscripts to Mozart's.

Sauguet

Bibliography

Baurraud, Henri, *Pour comprende la musique contemporaine*, Paris 1969.

Boulez, Pierre, *Penser la musique aujourd'hui*, Paris, 1963.

Boulez, Pierre, *Relevés d'apprenti*, Paris, 1966.

Busoni, Ferruccio Benvenuto, Writings and Letters (in German, Italian and English), Leipzig, 1907; Berlin, 1935; Florence, 1941; London, 1938; New York, 1911.

Casella, Alfredo, *L'evoluzione della musica attraverso la storia della cadenza tonale*, 1919, London, 1964.

Collaer, Paul, *Darius Milhaud*, Anvers, 1947.

Collaer, Paul, *La Musique moderne de 1905 à 1945*, Paris, 1955.

Collet, Henri, *L'Essor de la musique espagnole au XXème Siècle*, Paris, 1929.

Cortot, Alfred, *French Piano Music*, Oxford, 1932.

Dent, Edward, *Ferruccio Busoni, A Biography*, Oxford, 1933.

Debussy, Claude, *Monsieur Croche et autres écrits*, Paris, 1973.

Debussy, Claude, *Lettres à André Caplet*, Geneva, 1957.

Debussy, Claude, and Toulet, Paul-Jean, Correspondence, Paris, 1929.

Dukas, Paul, *Écrits sur la musique*, Paris, 1948.

Emmanuel, Maurice, *Pelléas et Mélisande*, Paris, 1926

Fauré-Frémiet, Philippe, *Gabriel Fauré*, Paris, 1927.

Gauthier, André, *Puccini*, Paris, 1961

Giazotto, Renato, *Busoni, la vita nell'opera*, Milan, 1947.

Goléa, Antoine, *Rencontres avec Messiaen*, Paris, 1960.

Bibliography

Hoérée, Arthur, *Albert Roussel*, new edition forthcoming.

Kœchlin, Charles, *Fauré*, Paris, 1927.

Lambert, Constant, *Music, Ho!*, London, 1934.
Lockspeiser, Edward, *Debussy*, two volumes, London, 1965.

Mellers, Wilfred, *Studies in Contemporary Music*, London, 1948.
Messiaen, Olivier, *Technique de mon langage musical*, Paris, 1944.
Moreau, Claire, À *la découverte d'André Caplet*, written in 1972, not yet published.
Myers, Rollo H., *Debussy*, London, 1948.
Myers, Rollo H., *Erik Satie*, London, 1948.
Myers, Rollo H., *Modern French Music*, London, 1971.
Myers, Rollo H., *Ravel; Life and Works,* London, 1971.
Myers, Rollo H., *Stravinsky*, London, 1950.

Nabokov, Nicolas, *Old Friends and New Music*, London, 1951.

Pahissa, J., *Vida y obre de M. de Falla*, Buenos Aires, 1947.

Roland-Manuel, Alexis, *Maurice Ravel*, Paris, 1914.
Roland-Manuel, Alexis, *Manuel de Falla*, Paris, 1930.
Rostand, Claude, *Entretiens avec F. Poulenc*, Paris, 1954.
Russolo, Luigi, *L'arte dei rumori*, Milan, 1916.

Schaeffer, Pierre, A *la recherche d'une musique concrète,* Paris, 1952.
Schaeffner, André, *Debussy et ses rapports avec la musique russe*, Paris, 1953.
Stravinsky, Igor, *Poétique musicale*, Paris, 1945.
Stravinsky, Igor, and Craft, Robert, *Conversations*, Volume I, London, 1959.
Stravinsky, Igor, and Craft, Robert, *Conversations*, Volume II, London, 1960.
Stravinsky, Igor, and Craft, Robert, *Conversations*, Volume III, London, 1962.
Suckling, Norman, *Fauré*, London, 1946.

Templier, Pierre Daniel, *Erik Satie*, Paris, 1932.

Valles, Léon, *Vincent d' Indy*, Paris, 1946–50.
Vlad, Roman, *Storia della dodecafonia*, Milan, 1958.

Xenakis, Iannis, 'Musiques formelles', Paris, *La Revue Musicale*, 1962.

Index

143

Index